Reflections:

the Stories and Life of a
COUNTRY VET

Robert Hirt, DVM

ISBN-13: 978-1517307127
ISBN-10: 1517307120

ACKNOWLEDGMENTS

I wish to acknowledge my good friend, Hans, for his computer savvy and his never-ending patience in helping me put together this manuscript.

I wish also to acknowledge both my surgeon, Dr. Lawrence Koep as well as Dr. Abraham Panossian for their intervening in a very serious health situation. Without either of them I might not be here to bring this work to fruition. And, last but not least, a huge thank you to my wife and lifelong partner, Patricia, the mother of my three children and indispensable helper in my country veterinary practice. Without their help this little book would not have been possible.

A Prayer For Animals

Hear our humble prayer, O God,
for our friends the animals,
especially for animals who are suffering;
for animals that are overworked,
underfed and cruelly treated;
for all wistful creatures in captivity
that beat their wings against bars;
for any that are hunted or lost or
deserted or frightened or hungry;
for all that must be put death.

We entreat for them all Thy mercy
and pity, and for those who deal with
them we ask a heart of compassion
and gentle hands and kindly words.
Make us, ourselves, to be true
friends to animals,
and so to share
the blessings of the merciful.

Albert Schweitzer

Table of Contents

THE GIFT

Fred was always complaining about his neighbors, his work, the weather, his poor crops, the economy and Lord knows, what else! He worked in a large steel plant as a foreman and I have no idea how he found time and the energy to own and operate his own dairy farm. Maybe that's why he always seemed so tired and cranky. Yet he felt he had to, to keep food on the table, and make ends meet. He had some 30 dairy cows and produced an average amount of milk but he was not, by any standards a great farmer. He never listened to any advice I offered about the health of his herd. On occasion he seemed to do just the opposite of what little advice I was able to ferret out to him. And he was always behind in paying his bills. On some days the bill incurred was double the installment he'd pay on the previous farm call. And on some visits he neglected to pay anything at all.

Unfortunately, farming for the average "Mom and Pop" operation has always been a rigorous challenge. Money coming in is just never enough to offset the up-front costs for grain, fuel, fertilizers, veterinary bills, etc., But these farmers accept all of this for the independence of being their own boss and being out in the fresh air of the country.

As one of six children of immigrant parents who eked out a living just to keep us hungry, growing kids fed I related somewhat to Fred. While not an immigrant, he too had a family of five–a couple of kids soon wanting to be going to college and one with a chronic health issue.

A couple of times as I drove past his farm at night Fred would be out there in the fields with his tractor with lights on, finishing up the last few acres that needed to be plowed. And then he would rush off to his day job at the plant.

But anyway, during the past few times while there, Fred would be watching me when I was finishing up and I'd be putting away my syringes and bottles of medicine, and cleaning up to move on to the next farm. He had that studied look on his face that bothered me–something was lurking in his brain.

"Doc, what d'ya call that thing you put all your stuff into ...that beat-up thing here that I'm lookin' at?"

"It's called a Pandora Bag" I said, half wondering what this was all leading to. Fred wasn't much for conversation but what he did say was rather intelligent in many ways. He wasn't big on kidding, and no dummy either and he was always wise about the day-to-day happenings of the world, the stock market, the price of milk, whatever.

I didn't see him for about a month and then six days before Christmas he asked me to come by to the farm.

"No rush, Doc–just when you're in the area, no special trip–I can't afford ya"!

We had a good working relationship, and I snickered to myself and muttered "just like old Fred"!

A few days later, while passing by his farm my curiosity got the better of me and I stopped in and tried to guess what

Fred wanted. It was unseasonably warm and the door to the milk house was open and I knew he was in there.

As I pulled in he heard me and sauntered out the door and said:

"I got a new baby here for ya, Doc, and this one ain't gonna cost ya nothin'...c'mon in."

And there it was, a new, hand-crafted Pandora Bag, made out of stainless steel–beautiful and shiny as a bottle. He had set it on a small table with a clean towel under it just to highlight the singularity of this gift. It had clever little knobs and drawers and a leather handle. You could see he had taken great pride in engineering this for me, exact measurements and all. He was proud as can be, like a little boy, offering up a gift to compensate for all those delinquent bills for the past year. Its value: probably well over $100.00 plus his labor of love and the great care that went into this very thoughtful gift.

"Merry Christmas, Doc" he said with a mischievous smile.

"And Merry Christmas to you, too," I muttered, half-smiling.

For whatever reason, the sun seemed to shine so very brightly for rest of the day.

* * * * * * *

Cows, Rabies
And Diverse Other Things

It was April in 1968 and I lived in a small village in Western New York State where I served as a veterinarian for many area dairy farmers. New York State is a very cosmopolitan state in that it boasts not only the gorgeous Finger Lakes region, the Rip Van Winkle area of the Hudson Valley, the Thousand Islands, the venerable Chautauqua Institution, Niagara Falls and the Big Apple, but also a thriving dairy industry. In fact New York State competes handily with the state of Wisconsin in numbers of dairy cattle. Several counties have more cattle than people.

My bride-to-be and I had set our wedding date for May 18th. She lived 45 miles away in the city. We had agreed to meet at City Hall–the 16th floor, to secure our wedding license. It was a sunny magnificent day to be a country veterinarian, and a workload not too large or potentially exhausting.

All went well as I whistled my way through a variety of tasks confronting me that day. Life was good. How could it not be with plans building for the big day of my wedding. Nothing could perturb me as the odometer clicked off a mere 74 miles. I was moving right along farm after farm, pleased with my work, my great relationship with my farmers. The ever-present thoughts of the "complete package" of a home, a satisfying career and a lovely bride and children with whom to share it all warmed me on that sunny but rather chilly April day.

My last farm stop was at Amos Yoder's. I had planned it that way. He had a few minor things for me to do–vaccinate some calves, treat a cow for a digestive problem–and then I'd be off for the rest of the afternoon to clean up and head to the city.

When I was about ready to clean my boots and head out Amos surprised me with a request: "Doc, you must come back to za pasture. I haf a dead cow zere and I vas told I haf to haf za head sent to za laboratory." My German heritage made me smile a little despite his sudden request for which I was not ready.

Rabies had been detected in that county a number of times in the past year and the only way it can be verified is by removal of the brain to examine a very small area for cells that are known as Negri bodies. I was not prepared for this at all. It was already getting late and I was in a dilemma. The head, once removed needed to be packed in ice and taken immediately to the State Laboratory. I had to first go to a McDonalds eight miles away to secure a couple of bags of ice. Removal of the head and packing it in ice was relatively easy.

A quick drive home, a quicker shower and a change of clothes and I was off to the city with that renewed feeling of comfort... a wedding in the planning as well as visions of my bride-to-be waiting for me there on that balmy afternoon. Of course, there was that cow's head in my back seat in an ice-filled 30 gallon garbage can!

The laboratory was in the very same building as the license bureau, only on a different floor, the 12th. I received a few stares carrying a garbage can in on the elevator but I was rather oblivious to it. This was approaching the finale... a great day to hold hands on the 16th floor with a sweet young thing who would be my bride one day very soon.

Dr. Peters was so enthusiastic about his work in the lab. One could easily tell he was right for this job. He exuded confidence, delighted in being a mentor and loved showing another professional what his work entailed. I followed his every step in the meticulous task of staining the brain tissue and finally subjecting it to careful scrutiny under the microscope.

"See those beautiful Negri bodies there?" he quizzed.

I did, but my mind was a bit fogged over at the moment. For awhile he had me wondering if I was in the wrong field. This was clean and exacting work and I was hooked!

And then it caught me by total surprise. I was here in City Hall for another reason!

"Oh, Dear God, will she still be there?" I thought. More than an hour had elapsed from the time I arrived at City Hall and our pre-arranged meeting time. I said my hurried goodbyes to the good doctor and was sweating bullets when I got to floor number 16. It seemed like forever getting there.

As I hurried to the licensing area no fewer than six people broke out in immediate applause. Dumbfounded, I later realized that I wouldn't be the first one to not show up for a signature that sealed the fate of an eligible bachelor. My wonderful sweet lady had a knowing smile for me… but I do believe that I detected a small tear in the corner of her eye.

* * * * * * *

Gypsy Lady

It was 5:00 AM and I couldn't sleep so I went out on my front porch in my PJ's to get some fresh air... to absorb the clearness of that early day in April. In the distance I could see a form coming slowly in my direction. In a few moments I was confronted by what appeared to be what is commonly referred to as a "bag lady." As she came closer to my porch she uttered something in a gravelly voice. Afraid that I'd miss what she had to say I stepped warily toward her.

"I know you," she said, "you're a vet, a cow doctor, or is it a pig doctor, eh?" A tone of sarcasm fell from her lips. "You're also the one who stole my lunch at the diner last week and I'm here to claim it!"

I had never seen this lady before and I began to wonder if this was an apparition of sorts because I hadn't been in Roscoe's Village Diner in well over ten years. Was I merely having a nightmare? I had never had a nightmare in my life so it couldn't be that. And, yes, there was the hint that she hadn't bathed in weeks and that made this apparition very real.

My wife, a very light sleeper, arose, came out to investigate and became alarmed immediately over this strange encounter.

"What's going on," she asked, "who is this person?" Now we were both bewildered. Why she picked our house instead of one of hundreds of others became a puzzle. Most likely she saw the light in our window. And evidently she knew the local vet lived here.

Then it dawned upon me: this was a new approach for a free meal, even at this early hour. It became evident that this MO–modus operandi–was a sure-fire way to quietly make the rounds of this community without fanfare and without drawing the attention of any neighbors.

We sat her down at a small outside table and gave her a cup of newly perked coffee and a sesame seed bagel with strawberry jam.

She gobbled it up as though she hadn't eaten in a week and then mumbled a quiet "Thanks and I sure hope you realize the error of your ways. Just don't go taking advantage of poor folks like me again!" And then she was gone.

A few weeks later her face was vaguely familiar in a patrol car at the traffic light on our street corner. And I always thought the panhandler at the corner of Main and Sycamore had a good thing going. I wonder where she got her training. She should check in with the local playwright–she's that good!

* * * * * * *

Dogs, A Pain–In The Heart!

My wife and I have no particular thought as to why we chose a black Labrador Retriever as our family pet. There are so many smaller "Benji-type" dogs out there that are adorable, easily cuddled, eat less and don't knock the chinaware off the table with their big, happy tails! Our choice for a name was Abigail, a name we picked before the puppy was even born. We loved the name and if we had another child we surely would have named her Abigail, or Abby for short.

Abigail was born on January 1, 1981. She had no idea who we were and had she known she might well have had something to say about the whole thing! When we brought her home at eight weeks of age "crating" was not yet popular, in fact it was barely heard of as part of the training program for puppies. As it turns out it is a wonderful, logical concept; it keeps the pup feeling secure in a close space, prevents all the messes created by an untrained puppy and furthermore, keeps the pup from chewing up and eating everything within eyesight and "sniff-site!"

We had four acres on which Abby could roam and feel free, under our control, of course. She loved to play as do all puppies. But as she grew up she seemed to favor baseball. I never did find out if she was a southpaw or not but she sure knew how to field the outfield slams. She never came back empty(mouth)-handed from out of the field and shrubbery after a line drive to center field. The time taken for her to retrieve the ball became directly proportional to her age–but she never failed even once, to do her job. Of course, that is why this breed is called retrievers!

Now when Abigail was two years old we decided to allow her to be a mother; not that she demanded it, in writing or anything of that nature. We just sensed that she would make a grand mommy. As a veterinarian I made sure she had no history of hip dysplasia based on radiographic evidence; similarly, the stud I picked out was subjected to the same regimen so as to greatly improve the chances of having puppies without that defect. All went well, with no problems in the entire planned pregnancy and Abby became the proud mother of eight puppies. She was a wonderful mother, not necessarily the greatest lactating queen, but attentive in every way possible. At eight weeks we found good homes for all eight, questioning prospective owners unmercifully about living arrangements. We instructed them about feeding times, bathing intervals, training and above all, being fully aware at all times, much like that of a child, of the pet's whereabouts. We'd shed a few tears as each pup left us, with the new owner assuring us that he or she was in good hands. It was not that easy to say goodbye to each roly-poly black bundle, but most certainly we had to.

The staff at the animal hospital had warm feelings for Abby when she was there for short stints of boarding or when she was there as a blood donor. I often wish that I had kept better records as to how many times she gave blood to a needy canine friend. And I suspect some recipients, if capable, would likely return to say "Thanks, I needed that!"

As she aged Abigail slowed down and became somewhat arthritic, possibly due to the vigorous athletic routine that she seemed to almost beg for daily through the years. As a seasoned veterinary acupuncturist I was able to bring considerable relief to our dear friend. She seemed to readily accept the twice-weekly routine on the select points of her body. She appeared to be more comfortable, ran more freely with enthusiasm that had seemed to pale months earlier. Slowly, we'd inevitably have to submit to the reality of her aging. Her eyes were becoming cloudy, the sign of developing cataracts; and her hearing was deteriorating as well. It was humorous to return home after an evening out and find her soundly snoring on the couch, on her back, with all four feet heaven-word. Normally, in earlier times she was banned from the couch but we strongly believe that she would wait to hear the garage door close when we'd leave and then immediately jump onto the place to which she thought she was entitled. So, as we arrived home she'd be sleeping like a princess, parents be-darned! When we'd awaken her she'd quickly jump off and give us that silly "grin" of guilt, upper teeth in full view, and head down for forgiveness. Apologies were not necessary.

Then, On November 7, 1996, the day of reckoning inevitably came. We knew it was time. Leaving the house, she had tumbled down three steps onto the garage floor. Unhurt, she got up, stood there shivering, seemingly asking: "What did I do wrong again this time?" It wasn't the first time and our hearts sank and we fell into each other's' arms, crying pathetically with deep sobs, both caressing our dear Abigail at the same time. It would be the very last time both of us would feel the depth of that dear creature's warm body. The vein found, death came peacefully as the euthanasia solution took its toll. For the next eighteen years Abigail's cremains sat silently on our dresser in an urn with her name proudly gracing the floral print on the cover. Fifteen years, ten months and seven days of love are not easily forgotten. These animals are such a pain... in the heart!

A Tribute To Abigail

I cried as I talked to her—quiet, solemn, deep talk.
No response was expected.
After so many years together there was an unspoken trust—borne of
mutual love and caring.
We had been to so many places together, covered so much territory,
experienced multiple joys and sadnesses in our separate lives.
I suspect both of us knew what lay ahead in that eternal abyss.

Those playful afternoons on the weekend in the backyard–
the blue-
watered pool that was solace from dripping sun–those silly
innocent
mistakes that bring thoughtless, instinctive reprimand.
And now the guilt, that painful day of reckoning, of decision that can no
longer be avoided; And then suddenly there they are–
poignant and
stabbing–the flood of memories and tears.
The time has come to say; "Good-bye my beloved friend. If
God has a
Heaven for furred creatures surely you'll be there."
God willing, I hope to someday look over there and see
you–totally
unaware of my presence, and fully immersed in play with
your
furry friends, those lovable Labrador Retrievers.

* * * * * * *

WAITING

We had agreed to meet outside under the huge orange archway above the entrance of the department store. She had only a five-minute errand and I was to not wander off somewhere and get lost! After all, we were in the intimates department and that was enough to confound me thoroughly.

We had only one cell phone. After all, why need two cell phones when one of us is usually home tending to other matters or reading a good book? Minutes dragged on, and on. I walked out to the car, drove down the long aisle and re-parked it, listened to music for a few minutes, got out and then headed toward that archway. My wife was nowhere to be found within my self-assigned radius of 100 feet, lest she pass me by and I would miss her completely. There was even a friendly-appearing wicker chair beckoning me to just "cool it" and re-lax–and wait, and maybe I'd even find a discarded magazine nearby to keep my spirits up and my dander down. It was stone-quiet at that entrance, but then a man came in by himself. He was walking with a profound limp and he was using a cane. He stopped for a moment, as if to rest and looked at me saying:

"I'll bet you're waiting for somebody, huh?" I nodded and he smiled,

"Yep, I know what that's all about!" He appeared to be in considerable discomfort so I offered him my chair and he gratefully accepted. It turns out he was a retired veterinarian from another state, visiting a son and two of his four grand-children. We chatted for almost thirty minutes about a few interesting episodes in his practice and I, in mine. We even shared a few laughs. The time literally flew by and it dawned upon me that I was still waiting for my wife!

Finally, concerned that maybe something was seriously wrong, I excused myself and went outside, going to the nearby corner of the store and looking toward another entrance. No luck. Now, there were two entrances to watch! I was hoping that while I was watching one she would not hurriedly scoot from the other into the parking lot to our car and then she would be waiting for *me*. I almost felt those death threats hanging over me! I attempted to settle down a bit.

And suddenly there it was–bright yellow–cruising by with a security gal at the wheel... a little golf cart with my wife in it, heading to the parking lot. "Oh, Dear God," I uttered to myself. "My existence will be forever in my own man-made purgatory!" I was out there staring absently into space and she heard me whistling one of my familiar tunes–one that she picked up immediately. She knows how often I whistle the same tune and instantly she turned her head and frantically yelled to the driver to stop.

"Where have you been?" were the very first words she uttered, half angry, half-glad to see me, half-crying, knowing that I had those very same concerns for her.

It seems I had dropped her off, expecting another boring wait while she was shopping without ever noticing *where* I was dropping her off. Then it all came out: She was at the other entrance, waiting for me. For the entire hour and then some, she paced and waited and worried.

How could I not have noticed that the two entrances are identical... huge orange-colored archways, differing only in the direction they face? Very briefly I stepped inside to say good bye to my new-found colleague. He then quickly offered why he was limping, probably because he knew I'd understand. He was seriously kicked by a horse years ago, followed by hip replacement surgery that failed and now, with his second new hip, he was optimistic for a full recovery. I wished him well with a smile and we said our good-byes.

It's really amazing how often you run into a colleague; sometimes in the damndest places.

* * * * * * *

THRESHING DAY

When the threshers came on a Monday morning we knew that they meant business. It was a glorious time for us kids because we knew we'd be around some folks that hadn't been to our farm in a year. We also knew from years past that this meant we boys would sit at the table with the *men* at lunch time when my mother and Grandma would cook up a feast for all the workers, and that included us. And boy, could we eat! It seemed like a Thanksgiving feast before Thanksgiving. There was two of everything: pork and beef, white potatoes and sweet potatoes, cranberry sauce, lots of bread with butter to lather on and then the pies. Oh, those pies!

Not only apple pie but mincemeat pie, and lemon meringue and at least six kinds of cookies. We even drank coffee to show everybody that we were like them. No one probably noticed how we screwed up the corners of our mouths before swallowing because at age 8 it took some getting used to.

Golly, we felt like *big men* on those days–the workers laughing and joking and eating heartily and we took it all in, pretending that we understood everything that was discussed from politics, and the weather to the price of milk and even how one of their cows managed a difficult birthing, with their expert help, of course!

I was born at a time when farmers relied on outside help to do the threshing of their grain crops. It would be unusual for a farmer to afford his own machinery to do this and thus there was a contingent of roaming threshers who would go from farm to farm, calculating in advance how many days were needed to finish the job there and move on to the next farm.

To this day I sport a scar on my wrist where my exuberant brother accidently slashed me while showing off his efficiency in dispatching the bundles of grain to the man feeding the hungry machine, one bundle at a time. We occasionally even got a reprieve from going to school for a day or two to help out. And that added to the sheer pleasure. Playing hooky probably came into being in exactly that way.

When we, a family of eight, moved some years later threshing for us was to become part of our family's memories. Modern advances in agriculture gave way to grain combines that roamed the fields and then the grain went to the barn or the bakery. Those golden days like that golden grain shall always be part of my being. It makes me proud to have been raised in times where work was very physical and its results were so very tangible.

* * * * * * *

HOLLYWOOD REJECT

It was in my Horoscope that day; I was destined to become a Hollywood star. The sun was brightly shining on that Saturday morning and my wife and I were in the city for an errand and some light shopping. As we rounded the corner of Spruce and High Street a crowd had gathered in front of Honors High School.

Honors is well known in the city of Buffalo, NY as a scholastically high caliber institution of learning. We found out in a few minutes that there were to be screenings for parts in the upcoming filming of "The Natural" of Robert Redford fame. Curiosity got the better of us so we got in line like everyone else and were finally ushered inside to seats. Two at a time they called us up to be photographed. The energy was there and I could just *feel* it. All the vibes spoke of my upcoming stardom. It was really palpable. It was amusing to see the photographer snip each Polaroid into two pieces to save paper. For Hollywood, of all places, where money never seems to be a deterrent to much of anything–that was a surprise.

Several days later the telephone rang and I would be a doctor, a walk-on extra. Already I could picture my name on the billings next to Robert Redford, Glenn Close, and Robert Duvall. And soon I'd have to have a chauffeur to drive me through the throngs of people on the premier of the showing! But first, I had to find a replacement to take my place at the animal hospital. Dr. James was between jobs and was eager to get his hands back into his chosen profession. I paid him the going rate and I was told he'd arrived on time, even early for his first day of work. The clients liked his manner; he was thorough and very adept at navigating through the new surroundings of the hospital.

Buffalo Psychiatric Center

The preparation for the part by the walk-ons was annoying and time- consuming; we had to get special haircuts, be fitted with straw hats, striped jackets, doctors' scrubs and were told to arrive at the shoot at precisely 8:15 a.m. Mr. Redford was late for the occasion. He disappeared into his trailer on the movie lot without ever so much as a "howdy" or a smile.

Now, much of the filming for what was to be Wrigley Field in Chicago was done at War Memorial Stadium in Buffalo and it was affectionately called The Old Rock Pile. It was a decrepit and seldom-used ball field in the old downtown section of the city. In fact, it was scheduled for demolition in the next couple of years to make way for a high rise apartment complex. It was there, I found out, that beyond the third row of real live spectators to the ball game were hundreds of paper people–cutouts of every size, color, race and gender; cutouts that looked so real and were so much cheaper and didn't ask for a paycheck. Now, Roy Hobbs the ballplayer, and the principal character of this movie, played by Robert Redford, was to be suddenly stricken with a severe illness in the game and was to be rushed to the nearest emergency hospital. In the film it was a nearby maternity hospital. Again, we were the attending "doctors" at the hospital and surrounding all of us were "pregnant ladies" waiting for their labor pains to signal that their time had come. I recall briefly taking a rest in a Director's chair. It turns out that the director's chair belonged to Barry Levinson, the director in this film. Somebody saw me sit down and yelled: "You can't sit there!" I was promptly ordered to vacate immediately! Mr. Levinson was a no-nonsense type of guy.

Now, in the movie the H.H. Richardson Towers, part of the State University at Buffalo campus, became the maternity hospital. The elegance of this magnificent piece of Buffalo's architecture is hard to describe. Built between 1871 and 1895 the Towers were originally part of the Buffalo Psychiatric Center. Left to deteriorate for many years, neglect rapidly took its toll. For the filming only one long hallway was restored to its original luster. We were told that it took weeks of intense labor to paint walls and ceilings, polish floors, install new lighting and general repair to make the area ready for filming.

It was then I found out that a real doctor, an endocrinologist from Buffalo, was to play the part of one of the staff doctors in the film. He had already been a veteran in another Buffalo-originating film, Best Friends, starring Goldie Hawn and Burt Reynolds.

As for me, I never uttered a single word in the movie, never saw myself anywhere in the many "takes," and ended up on the "cutting room floor"! I was never to see myself in the shiny lights of Hollywood! Perhaps I was the wrong type of doctor! And, to top it off, what I received as payment was exactly one-half of what I agreed to pay my replacement veterinarian. Maybe one day there'll be another movie filmed in Buffalo and I'll get another chance at stardom!

In all reality, I felt so much more comfortable in my world of animals and with the caring staff that worked with me for several years at my animal hospital. It was just good to be home again.

* * * * * * *

THE SLEIGH RIDE

I was coming home from an early morning call from Amos Miller's place after checking out a goat that had lost a lot of blood on a barb wire fence that he managed to get snared around his back leg. He helped me to restrain the animal, clean the wound out and dress it, with orders to keep it separated from the rest of the animals for a week. He was good about following advice and was generally a good client even though I saw him only a couple of times a year.

On the way home I saw a crowd gathering at a yard sale. It was at another farm and I knew the owner even though he wasn't a client. Nevertheless I stopped by, just being nosey to see what old Frank had to sell. Turns out it was not only a yard sale but a full-fledged estate sale and it proved very interesting to me. He had old horse harnesses and collars and a surrey that looked like it came from the historic *Gone With the Wind* movie. Behind it and partially hidden by old barrels and two step ladders of pre-World War II vintage was a creaky old sleigh, the one-horse kind. It had a dusty black leather retractable canopy complete with a small round window on each side. All it needed was a horse to pull it, which wasn't part of the package. The canopy's interior was lined with red velvet. Clearly, it had seen a few mice in its day and the droppings on the floor of the sled affirmed that right away. The sleigh had real possibilities to my way of thinking!

I went to the cashier and inquired about it. She said; "Sorry, that's been sold."

I looked back dejectedly at the sleigh and saw a man fiddling with part of the leather seat inside. I walked over, asked him if he knew who bought the sleigh, figuring it was probably him.

He said gruffly: "My wife bought the damn thing and now I gotta drag it home. Don't know what she had in mind but it's one more piece of junk I need like a hole in the head."

That raised my spirits a bit.

"I'll take it off your hands if you're interested," I offered, hoping his wife wasn't around. I already knew what he paid for it and offered him twenty -five dollars more than he paid and he took it without any hesitation at all. I didn't want to be around when his wife came out from the house!

I returned later that day with my pickup and with help loaded it and took it home to my barn. My wife seemed delighted with my purchase but immediately retorted; "Well, all we need now is the horse!"

I had a brain storm of sorts then and said; "You watch, I have it all figured out!"

It was a slow day the following Saturday and I made a device that took the horse out of the picture completely: I made it in such a way that I could hook the pole of the sleigh to my farm tractor and we'd be all set.

My daughters were totally embarrassed as they sat with my wife on that snowy Sunday evening in January being regally escorted round and round in the neighborhood in a one-horse open sleigh. It had a red lantern hanging from the backside and a strap of bells clinking from one of the side rails. In time the girls got over the serious trauma that I caused in their lives on that snowy night! They occasionally remind me of it when they reflect on the rural lifestyle we enjoyed back then.

* * * * * * *

THE TRAP LINE

Making a few bucks as youngsters seemed overly important to us three boys back East. Never mind the three girls... they were on their own and probably never felt the "power" and prestige of having a few coins jingling in their pockets. We three boys, ages seven, ten and eleven years old at the time, wanted money desperately, for whatever reason I have no earthly idea. Anyway, on a recent trip to see how the young cattle were doing in the distant pasture, Dad had noticed that the muskrats were making a thorough mess of the creek bank and maybe we should be trapping them to reduce their numbers. Besides, the girls had no stomach for any of this "trapping stuff," leave alone getting out of bed at 4:30 a.m. and trudging the two miles of a trap line, dispatching of our booty and craftily setting the traps for yet another day. We learned fast; we three would alternate days, always two of us being together to brave the darkness and fetch home our bounty. Some days were especially prolific... five to seven animals, dead of course, slung over our shoulders, when a mere twelve or thirteen traps were all we had set to start with. Some days, of course, we came home empty handed, disgruntled, still tired and now only half-hungry for our breakfast, for we had eaten most of the apple or carrot pieces that were to have been used for bait but now no longer needed.

Muskrat boards are about two feet long and tapered from eight inches wide down to a point.

Cleverly crafted by some old artisan, they serve as drying boards for the inverted skins. After a week or so of drying, the skins are taken to merchants who huckster them out to furriers who then assemble dozens of the best quality skins into muskrat coats. I sometimes wonder if we ever even considered the possibility of contracting some strange disease carried harmlessly by these little animals.

One time a neighbor stopped by to inform us of a dying cow in that same distant pasture. He had observed while driving by that it hadn't moved in many hours and that something must be wrong. Those were the kind of concerned neighbors we all love to have. We got the animal home, and after some curious "poking around" by us kids my Dad called our veterinarian. After discussing various possibilities he entertained the thought of rabies and after the animal's demise he removed the head and had the animal checked for this dread disease. Diagnosis: positive. And to think we kids had no idea of the potential disaster this could have wrought upon our family. We had no way of knowing. No thought was ever given to any preventive measures. How we all exposed ourselves with such carelessness still astounds me to this day. Thankfully, we all survived.

Life goes on and we all change, usually for the better, and we find more profitable and pleasurable endeavors. But then we stop to reminisce and recount the simple things that made us happy at the time.

Nostalgia, in proper measure, can be such an all-encompassing and beautiful word!

* * * * * * *

ANOTHER WORLD

Our plane stumbled to a bumpy stop just before take-off on the pot-holed tarmac in Bangkok. We were told there were engine problems so off we went to the (only) other plane there that took us to Ching Rai in Northern Thailand. As we landed a small contingency of mostly curious children, some smiling, others wearing that bewildered, sometimes frightened look, greeted the seven of us as our hosts escorted us to the small thatch-roofed huts on the outskirts of this bustling city. The next morning, after sleeping on mats, the crowing of the only rooster in all of the city reminded us at 4:00 a.m. that it was time for him and for us to rise and shine. We obeyed, even though the forthcoming orange globe in the Eastern sky hadn't even hinted that a new day was about to begin.

Heifer International had visited its largesse in the form of animals upon this poor but colorful land of gentle people. We were informed of the great strides this wonderful organization had made in trying to alleviate poverty, one family at a time, not only here but in over 125 countries.

We all sat Indian style on the plank floors as the village elder, a wizened man with his silvery beard, spoke to us through an interpreter about all the female goats that found a new home in this superbly efficient program that was begun by a single benevolent man, dairy farmer Dan West, over 65 years ago in the United States. Now some 20 species of animals round out the list of Heifer International's giving program geared to the needs of families from Bulgaria to Brazil and from Kentucky to Kosovo. Over 13.5 million families have been given an opportunity to better their lives since Heifer's inception in 1944.

We, a group of several veterinarians and two ministers, spent the better part of a morning on a river motoring towards a Padaung village to see the long-necked women so ornately "on display," and perhaps to part with a few coins for the privilege. The brass rings adorning their legs and their necks signify a coming of age for the females. In reality their anatomy is grotesquely manipulated over time as their shoulders sag to accommodate these rings. This small colony, really refugees from Burma, now Myanmar, makes its meager living from their own crops and the few precious coins from foreigners that arrive there strictly by boat. There are no autos, no roads, no bicycles.

Next, we winged our way over Cambodia to Vietnam, landing in lovely Saigon, now known as Ho Chi Min City. The French influence is so evident there especially at the ornate Hotel Continental where our troops in the war stayed for R&R before returning to battle. Nearby, it struck me as uniquely funny that I was invited by a local youngster, with a generous spirit and a bigger smile, to engage in an impromptu tennis match. Happily, no language barrier existed there whatsoever. What a treat!

We then motored by improvised raft down the Mekong River to a gentleman farmer's estate where we were treated to a delicate meal of rabbit, fish, sticky rice and gravy. En route it was not unusual to see human effluent and toilet tissue floating while children playfully swam nearby.

Though not a recipient of a Heifer gift this farmer had heard of our arrival and had his staff prepare a welcome lunch. Again, we experienced the goodness of these kind and gentle folks, something the average tourist may not be privy to.

Those 18 days in another world gave me insight as to the privilege of being an American but also to the kindness, generosity and warmth of strangers on the other side of our planet. Regarding the sometimes annoying discomforts endured and the plethora of enlightening experiences I might very well label this the "best and the worst" of any travel experience in my life.

* * * * * * *

TURKEYS, TURKEYS

Turkeys are part of America's heritage. Known by geneticists as Meleagris gallopavo, these birds are seen over much of North America and Canada.

We had seen turkeys numerous times on our property... as many as ten or twelve staying pretty much together as a flock and dispersing immediately when threatened by unusual noise or by movements. We've seen them fly high over the tops of sixty to seventy foot tall pine trees, disappearing into the yonder only to be seen again the next day on our acreage. Considered very alert with keen hearing capabilities these birds thrive in the wilds of the cooler climates, especially of the Northeast. Occasionally they wander into the more residential areas to the delight of suburban folks, especially when they "strut their stuff" so very colorfully.

As our three children were growing up we decided to instill a sense of responsibility and a good work ethic into them. I recall how as a teenager my brother and I each raised turkeys for market and in the process made some pocket change for ourselves. We did this for several years enjoying what we felt was *our* project, a chance to break out of the demands of rigid work-oriented German parents.

We hammered together boards and wire and tin roofing scraps to fashion a turkey pen, all the while keeping our eyes on the prize that was to be there five months later when Thanksgiving rolled around. Unfortunately, some clever weasels found their way into the pen one night and chewed the heads off of a number of them. Not to be discouraged we started over again being more careful to secure their digs.

When our children were old enough to be more responsible we bought fifteen one-day old turkey poults for them to learn what responsibility is about in a big way. This time they had a pen that kept the weasels out! They initially loved the idea. They'd rotate the chores amongst themselves so that only one had to go down to the barn to feed them and let them out. It was fun and a few of the birds even had peculiar names. How they could tell one from the other totally baffled us parents.

One bird became so hungry for his lunch that he started pecking at another one, drawing blood. We found out who the culprit was by the blood on his beak. We called him "the carnivore!" Birds are notorious cannibals and unless severe actions are taken they will kill the victim or victims. We had seen this many years earlier in our flock of chickens.

Now, from June 10th until November 22nd is a very long time. Week by week the chore became less of an adventure. And slowly it became a "drag!" They'd carry on and moan and grumble, especially at night when homework needed to be done and by the occasional parental warning to "get out there and put the turkeys back into the barn and feed them!" Thanksgiving couldn't come fast enough for them. Dad had the responsibility of slaughtering them and dressing them out for market, a job I had done before but still did not relish. It was

Time and high school faded into the distance and life went on... to marriage and fatherhood and a satisfying career. Looking back into the mirror of time was, and still is, a joy of sorts.

For many years my baseball bat was lost. I looked for it everywhere every time I returned home. And then finally it happened on a return visit back to the family farm many years later. It stood there silently in a corner of our cavernous barn, a structure that reeked heavily of stale cow manure. There it was, disheveled and tired-looking in its own way. There were deep grooves and chinks out of its exterior. In a ray of sunlight I caught sight of the huge cobweb glistening from its handle and extending over to the nearby window sill. It was almost as though it cried out that it needed resurrecting and one more chance to be some kid's friend.

But now, I had a son who, at this early age knew exactly what a baseball bat was for. With renewed dedication I brought it back to life on my lathe down in our basement, albeit half its original size. I sanded it and polished it with the love and affection that only a loving parent can have. And now, many years later, my son has a gift for his son to reflect upon.

* * * * * * *

Dog Owners vs. Dog Lovers

There's always that temptation to form an opinion; it's life and part of the "human condition," a phrase I've never liked to use or see in print and yet I find it appropriate here. For example, some dog owners relish their dogs for the love they bring into a family. They are indeed *part* of the family. Their ultimate demise due to the infirmities of old age, accidental death, whatever, compares with the loss of any other family member. The grief is very real and the void lingers often for weeks, maybe for years. The owners often recite stories of joy or sadness much like those after the loss of a child.

Then there are the "people who own a dog," period. What utilitarian favors they may return... hunting, protecting property, eating leftover foods, whatever, is fine and that's it! They appear to see no warmth or value in companionship, given or received by that animal... its existence in that household is merely a fact of life. Oftentimes it's reflected in the name given to the animal, such as "Stupid" or "Shit head," never anything endearing at all. Those kind of pet owners are not the usual, thankfully, but nevertheless they do exist.

One pet owner I distinctly remember was the one who brought in "Fat Stuff" with a broken leg. He insisted that he could put a splint on the leg and all would be okay but "I thought I'd give you a shot at it, Doc ...I just ain't got the time to mess with it."

All went well and I felt pleased with the surgery as well as the cast placed on the leg. Two days later when Fat Stuff came in for a re-check the staff remarked on the horrendous odor coming from the dog. In the exam room I questioned Bill about the homecare given and the restrictions placed on this surgical patient.

"Doc, he loves to be outside most of the day; he lays in the mud puddle by the back porch and hates to come up, even for his favorite soup bones. I just don't understand it no how...."

What the devil was this guy thinking? The poor animal had to be admitted and the cast removed, of course, under heavy sedation, the leg thoroughly cleansed and disinfected and finally, the leg re-cast. A multitude of prayers were silently proffered by us at the hospital and our client was again on his way later in the day with some stern warnings. The Good Lord must have been with us on that occasion for infection of the bone is common with such gross contamination, despite a massive regimen of antibiotics. The bone healed without any complications.

Then there was the huge Mastiff that was hit by a Volkswagen. He had jumped from the back of the man's pickup truck while on the highway. I chuckled to myself, wondering what the Volkswagen must have looked like in that encounter. The dog, Bozo, came in happily wagging his tail, sniffing everyone in the reception area with great delight while the owner was just slightly concerned.

"Doc, I'm on the way to work and I have to have this tear in his chest fixed up," said Mike, very nonchalantly. "My wife's outta town so she can't pick him up. I'll leave work a little early and stop by to pick him up just before closing time," never asking if that was going to be okay or if the dog would be ready to be discharged.

Normally, one thinks about risks of general anesthesia in a "shocky" patient but those signs were just not there. Bozo was just a happy dog that would, if allowed, lumber around the whole animal hospital with not a care in the world. He greeted everyone within reach of the 10 feet of the dirty rope that tethered him to his oblivious owner.

Wanting to be a good guy and to accommodate his master I relented and weighed the odds of this 207 pound hulk going into shock. We proceeded with an I.V. drip, slowly inducing general anesthesia. All went well in the surgical department, beautiful stitch line and all. As I was finishing up I was suddenly taken aback by a *very* significant fact: the dog had stopped breathing while the technician had turned her back. His membranes were now very pale. I called for the surgical tech to remove the gas machine and breathe for the dog. We were confronted with a potentially expired patient. All the remedies at our disposal in such situations were attempted. None worked.

I forced myself to not panic. Then the Brain Storm: The window air conditioner had been turned on to keep the surgical suite a bit cooler. Almost reflexively I yanked the cord out from it leaving two bare wires staring at me. "What are you doing?" cried Jan, the technician, scared half to death at what I was going to do. I split the wires far enough apart and touched each front paw with one end of a live wire. Nothing... maybe a small twitch of the legs. I did it again... and then again! Magically, this time the animal gave a huge sigh and started breathing again. The rest is history; the dog made a complete recovery and was later sent home.

"How'd everything go, Doc?" asked Mike.

"Reasonably well," I said wondering if all the raw emotions of that experience poked through onto my countenance. "That big guy sure has a lot of grit," I said. Mike would never know how many gray hairs came onto my scalp that day!

Two months later we had the misfortune of admitting this beautiful dog again... this time, sadly, as a corpse. Bozo had jumped from the back of the owner's pickup truck onto the expressway and was killed instantly by a tractor trailer.

Go figure.

* * * * * * *

Hornless And Unhappy

In most dairy herds it has become standard practice to remove the horns of cattle to prevent disfiguring fighting, the loss of an eye or other injuries, or even bullying of their peers. One can easily picture a Texas Longhorn species goring a victim by the feed trough just to gain advantage. Now, for humanitarian reasons alone it is considered appropriate to remove the horns of cattle when they are under six months of age and then only when a local anesthetic is first injected. Sadly though, adult animals are sometimes sold and if the original owner did not follow through and have the dehorning process done when the animal was a youngster that animal will likely again try to establish its "hierarchical position" in its new home. Thus, the need in many cases to dehorn an adult bovine.

Such was the case when Leonard called me to his farm to treat a dairy cow that was not eating properly and was acting strangely, bobbing its head frantically. The cow had been dehorned.

"Doc, Casey came over the other day. He told me that he's done this many-a-time and it ain't a problem–told me he'd done another neighbor's awhile ago and that's what friends are for!" The neighbor, not wanting his friend to incur a veterinary fee, used a saw to remove the horns. On adult cattle there is often an open cavity remaining after the horn is removed. Normally this cavity should be covered until a natural seal develops. Leonard hadn't thought of that and thus hay seeds and grain from a neighboring bovine heavily contaminated the surgical site. The sinus cavity became grossly infected and the poor cow was in considerable pain. Any attempt to flush the site was met with obvious discomfort. Even a local anesthetic did little to dull the pain. Within two minutes the beast let out a horrific roar, broke free of its stanchion, backed up and galloped full speed down through the center of the barn.

She was not to be subdued. Leonard headed her off but, not to be outdone she turned and reversed her direction. This time she seemed even more intent on avenging the cruelty she must have felt was perpetrated upon her body. With no hesitation whatsoever she plowed into and through my open medical case standing in the aisle. Not quite content that she had done enough damage she again reversed direction and headed back and one more time adorned the case with samples of urine and manure as she ran.

Lenny said to me: "Doc, the hell with her, let her settle down and come back tomorrow and maybe by then what little you were able to do today will have helped some." We both smiled through our sweaty faces, and went on to another job in the next barn, one that allowed us to cool off and thank the Good Lord that we humans were born without horns. Leonard seemed sheepish, maybe even a little embarrassed during the rest of my time there. What could I say?

* * * * * * *

Pioneer Spirit

October Hill Farm was borne of Germanic people, immigrants from their homeland of southern Germany. Silas and Rebecca were our newest friends back east who, after marriage emigrated from the Bavarian region to our Land of Plenty.

Although almost total strangers to this country they envisioned a new start in life, a start with offspring that also would embrace hard work and a desire to be independent. They told us that over time, America may well become a real and actual home-away from home for them. We hoped so.

Relatives in Offenbach gave them just enough money to get a good start and when the horizon looked more favorable they would happily start to repay them. Silas envisioned that one day soon they'd put money down on the little house they were now renting. Money started coming in slowly at first from their laying hens, and later from the vegetable garden that they planted and fastidiously groomed and nurtured on a daily basis.

But early on problems started to come along. Sickness in their young twin children began to occupy much of their time, their energy, and seriously drain their meager funds. Their enthusiasm began to wane in the ensuing months. Sarah, a twin, seemed constantly on death's doorstep. Within four months of their arrival in the country she was hurriedly taken to the hospital on three separate occasions. Would the other twin be next?

The couple just loved how their little home stood on a grassy knoll. They could look out from the kitchen window and see pastures and croplands for miles around. Not far from the home was a beautiful stand of yellow pine at the edge of the property. The owners actually gave them access to the timber saying:

"We ask that you cut down only what you need for repairs of the barns and hen house; and there's a sawmill in the next village." How generous of these kind people. They remembered the days when they too were immigrants.

Ten months after they moved onto the property a ferocious storm came unexpectedly into the area. Luckily, the little house only shook and rattled but withstood the hammer-like blows of a gale-force wind that seemingly came from nowhere. They clung to each other, fearful that Satan surely was visiting. At dawn, looking westward toward the forest they saw all the up-rooted trees. By the hundreds they were lying much like a battery of soldiers cut down en masse by a torrent of bullets, eerily solemn, and now waiting for the woodsman's ax. They lay in a perfectly geometrical pattern. Ultimately, they'd be at the mercy of the forces of nature and their branches would slowly begin to melt into the earth. It had only been a year ago that another forest not far from there had met its own sad demise.

Hildo Island, only a few miles from them, known by many as a paradise of serenity and green, was once again warning newcomers of the sudden danger that awaits unwary residents. Residents had no idea of the ever changing weather patterns of that little island.

It was now Spring and the proprietor of another farm, also not far from this small stand of trees, had himself experienced the ravages of nature, the fate of such overwhelming destruction by that same violent act of nature. He had lost two barns, a silo and worse, the death of five animals lying sleepily under a huge oak tree. The tree came down with no warning whatsoever when a wind of immeasurable force announced itself just hours before sunrise.

And then also, two years earlier four other cattle met their fate as well under still another tree when lightning struck as they lay together, sleepily, rhythmically chewing their cuds. Each time a veterinarian had to be summoned to verify the cause of death so that insurance might partially reimburse the distraught farmers.

On autopsy in cattle certain features point toward death by electrocution. It was a huge loss, for the value of these animals was one thing, but the loss of a monthly milk check was quite another. When one understands that a dairy cow can produce forty or more pounds of milk daily it amounts to a considerable loss in the monthly milk check.

Prayerfully, this young couple accepted their fate, knowing full well that there were others, who had it so much worse... heart problems, cancer and crippling injuries from farm accidents. They knew prayer and the Lord answered in kind, sparing them their sweet twins with the tenacity to bounce back from sicknesses that seemed to be never-ending. Things were starting to level off.

And then Silas came upon a fortunate situation: Would he be willing to oversee a farm and the stock in a nearby pasture? The woman, Beatrice, herself in failing health had recently lost her husband. Left alone, the farm would go into rapid decline and would then have to be sold off. It had been in the family for over 120 years. Such an opportunity does not present itself frequently. Silas jumped at the chance. Not only was he offered a fair stipend but a yearly side of beef for his family's consumption. And then, as good fortune would have it, Rebecca found that her rug-hooking expertise had brought her somewhat of a nice reputation in the area. She absolutely loved doing it as well; she referred to it as a labor of love. The income from that little hobby would also help pay the bills and fill the larder for the next winter. A penny earned is a penny saved.

Silas and Rebecca were a team in every sense; they worked so very hard but enjoyed their Sundays fully. Their church became a staple of their lives. Silas soon became a deacon.

One can say that this is the true American story of young immigrants who knew what they wanted and, expected no handouts... no entitlements. They believed that the fabric of good living dictated being part of a community, being conscientious, honorable and having a deep sense of integrity. And such was part and parcel of early America, from the Pilgrim ships at Plymouth Rock to the expansion of the colonies, and eventually the territories that eventually became the states, now fifty in number. This is early America: one pilgrim family at a time.

* * * * * * *

IN-UTERO OR EX-UTERO?

The surprising jangle of my telephone pulled me from a good book I was reading. It was 7:30 p.m. on a February night in rural New York State. In a country veterinary practice one gets fairly accustomed to this but it never sits well to be out after dinner hour. One can bet it will be a real emergency situation. Occasionally there will be two back-to-back calls and that often means dragging oneself back home close to midnight, weary and wet. No one ever said large animal practice would be easy.

"Doc, my cow 'cast her wethers,'" said Dave on the phone, all out of breath. The term is known typically by dairy farmers and veterinary practitioners alike. But, as a farm kid and having the situation occur at our farm several times many years ago I knew exactly what "casting her wethers" was all about. Simply put it means that while giving birth to a calf the entire uterus will be pushed out through the birth canal to the outside. Correctly stated, it is a prolapse of the uterus and it occurs occasionally.

When I arrived at the farm a huge truck was just leaving the driveway as Dave was heading toward the barn. I noticed the Florida license plate on the truck's rear bumper. "Doc, take a taste of this orange. I've never tasted anything so sweet!" It appears that the truck and its driver had been making the rounds of the country farms selling these Florida oranges. And indeed they were the sweetest I had ever tasted.

Before even entering the barn to see the poor cow I said to Dave, "Bring me a five-pound bag of your wife's sugar, okay?" Dave had no idea what this bag of sugar had to do with fixing his cow but he happily complied, still sucking on the last quarter of the Florida orange.

One should try to picture a prolapsed uterus of the bovine. It is roughly the size of the 24 to 26 inch inflated balls seen in gyms and are used to strengthen one's back muscles... only more slippery and bloodier. Now comes the task of replacing this gargantuan organ, for if left out the animal will surely die. One must first administer an epidural of lidocaine to quiet the reflexive contractions of the reproductive tract during labor. That achieved, the sugar is literally dumped all over the uterus. The sugar will almost immediately absorb liquid and cause shrinkage of the engorged mass... and rather dramatically! Then, with the assistance of the farmer holding up a tray holding the uterus the veterinarian can slowly force the uterus through the birth canal into its normal position in the animal's body.

Dave, all sweaty from the exhaustive effort of holding that tray with its uterus managed a wan smile and likely wondered what might come next! We were mostly done. With antibiotics inserted deep into the cavity the problem will usually be resolved. Within several months it will again be ready for the next pregnancy

"Dave, check her in an hour and again at about two in the morning. If by milking time she appears okay she'll likely be fine.

"By the way, did you buy that peddler's oranges"? I queried.

"Yep, bought two bushels."

"Great," I said. "How are they?"

"They're the worst damn oranges I've ever tasted in all my born days," he said.

The oranges that the peddler brought out for tasting evidently were spiked with a sugar solution hours before the sampling was to occur. Small syringes with an ultra-fine needle are used to inject a sugar solution into the orange. A roving sheriff deputy informed me of this scam foisted upon the local farmers. A ring of these culprits was caught in another county last year. Live and learn, I guess.

* * * * * * *

LAUNDRY DAY

Laundry day came at least once a week for my poor frazzled mother. But she tackled that chore with a vengeance, never stopping the sorting, pre-scrubbing and finally teasing the heavy clothes through the wringer.

We wore overalls back then, now referred to as jeans. But no matter what they were called they always smelled dirty, covered with cow barn "stuff" and usually with wet cuffs and often with torn-out knees.

I really hated those days, mostly because you couldn't walk through the kitchen without stumbling over a pile of dirty clothes. And it felt as though that wringer washer indeed claimed its right to be right there in the middle of the floor churning away dutifully and seeming to say brashly: "today is *my* day, so clear out and let me do my job"!

On hot summer days she'd do the wash on the back porch where it was cooler. Mama always used Fab. That was the only thing I really tolerated in my brain… the pleasant smell of that detergent. But the sight of that wringer turning scared me too, mostly because I was afraid my mother would someday get a hand caught or be pulled into it unmercifully with nobody there to help free her. I could just imagine her all flattened out lying on the floor.

One year our cousin, Georgie, came up from the city to be with us kids for a week. He was a big windbag type of guy… always bragging about everything he knew that we kids, ages eight, ten and eleven should know about. He brought his Savage.22 rifle along to show us how to shoot. *We* knew how to shoot but we never let on because we wanted to show him up a bit. After all, we were dumb country hicks that had to be taught everything!

Then the time came to hang out the wash on my grandma's line at the back of the house next to the grapevine. She shared the wash line with my mother.

When my mother and grandma went back into the house Georgie said; "Here's a good place to practice shooting. After we're done here you can go out and kill a woodchuck or a skunk with a single shot." Wow, we could be that good?

So Georgie hung a tin can on the wash line, dangling it down about twelve inches to make it more of a moving target. We boys would take turns, first Tommy, then Al and finally me. But, of course, first he had to give us a demonstration how it should be done. He took no fewer than 6 shots; Georgie looked like a real pro with that familiar swagger and cocky manner.

Wow, we thought; "this guy's really good!" that is until we ran down to see the damage to the tin can; we laughed out loud and mocked him out. There was only a single hole in the can.

Tommy and Al got their chances too but were able to put only one more hole in the tin can. Now came my turn.

"You're not big enough to shoot that thing so maybe you should wait 'til next year," he said sarcastically. But he wasn't holding the gun.

Al gave it to me and whispered, "Show that asshole a thing or two!" I'd never shot a .22 rifle before so it was a new experience for me. Al said : "Be careful, it's got a kick to it; hold it tight to your shoulder."

That done, I took careful aim and pulled the trigger very carefully. All the shirts and overalls instantly fell to the ground. I had shot the main wash line in half and in the pile of rubble on the ground was the tin can.

"Grandma will kill me," I muttered! With just one bullet I had become a genuine marksman!

"What the hell's the matter with you!" said Georgie; "you're supposed to aim at the tin can."

We laughed and gloated for a half hour and Georgie had gotten his come-uppance. Of course, we three boys all knew that when "push came to shove" I hardly knew which end of the gun did the damage.

Georgie never offered to teach us anything after that. In fact, he never came back to the farm again and said he was just too busy. Darn.

* * * * * * *

Rain, Rain, Go Away? (Maybe Not!)

Honeymoons are supposed to be like milk and honey, literally! When we traveled to Florida many years ago to prepare for our marital bliss it never occurred to us that even then, in its fledgling state, marriage can start off on the wrong foot. Our plans were altered as we went along, sometimes by the weather, and sometimes by other circumstances.

When we left the church smiling and with devil-may-care attitudes, we had no idea what lurked in front of us. Indeed, most of us don't. When we left the church it started to rain– hard, driving rain that made guests huddle under umbrellas and occasionally look skyward for some sign of relief. But it didn't come. Nor did it come the next day or the next day after that.

En route to Florida the sun teased us a little here and there but the rains never gave up. Neither of us was aware that the other used any swear words until then. It was a profound surprise and an indoctrination of the two of us to a vocabulary that gained momentum as the rain marched on, day after day. Underneath it all we laughed heartily as another new word spilled out to the chagrin of the other. We were on our honeymoon!

We got to the hotel in Miami Beach and the sun flirted again with us, briefly. After getting settled in our room, wanting some cold tap water we were surprised to find that there was no water. It had been turned off, briefly, we were told to repair a broken water main in the parking lot. That turned into 6-hour "briefly!" That was okay though—we were on our honeymoon!

I asked my lovely bride to join me for a swim but she declined so off I went off to the beach.

The sun had finally found us and things were looking up. I thought it strange that the beach was so barren of people on this lovely day. Paddling around in five to seven feet of water and just looking askance I was puzzled that I was alone. Surely not everyone was at work! All of a sudden a horrible whirring sound, frightening just by its unusual pitch, enveloped the air space around me. And then I saw it: a school of fish–literally hundreds, flying in a rainbow-like arc near me and heading toward shallow waters. Totally puzzled, I was scared and almost instinctively swam toward shore as fast as I could. What was this all about? It was then that I saw an elderly couple sitting in folding chairs on top of a break wall. Our eyes met. "Did you see that? I asked. "Sure did" came the response, matter-of-factly. "What do you make of it," I asked. "Didn't you see the sign: NO SWIMMING TODAY-SHARK WARNING?" he said, equally matter-of-factly. Truth be told, I hadn't. *Must be the honeymoon daze,* I thought. I returned to the hotel white as a ghost. I don't think my wife believed a word of my story. I invited her to an interview with the elderly couple but she declined.

Days moved on, St. Petersburg Beach, a friendly warning by a patrol officer who couldn't keep up with me. No matter;

we were on our *Honeymoon*! Before leaving Florida I took my new wife to a laboratory in Kissimmee where I spent some time seven years earlier as a summer employee of the Department of Agriculture. Under the supervision of a field veterinarian we had blood tested over fifteen thousand dairy cattle on several huge dairy operations. I was saddened to learn that many animals on these farms were destined for slaughter because they were carriers of brucellosis, a disease that causes undulant fever in humans. It was a very valuable and worthwhile program and I felt good to be a part of it.

We next flew to New York City. It rained there also, of course. The theatre, the restaurants, the excitement; it was all lovely. But it never stopped raining! My sister, Ginny, a nurse at a large hospital there put us up for three days. The honeymoon was coming to an end. It rained en route to Albany, my old hometown. The visit and family closeness was just wonderful. But work was awaiting at the other end, in western New York, my wife's hometown. And it rained some more as we drove the final 300 miles. But–we were *still* on our honeymoon.

When we arrived in western New York and at our new home the sun was shining brightly. Some 47 years later we look back with a smile and think about the omen about rain on the wedding day and honeymoon. It appears that it's true!

* * * * * * *

FAME FROM OUT IN THE STICKS

We all know the famous face of Abraham Lincoln, our sixteenth president, a man known to this very day for his integrity, for his rise from poverty to becoming a learned scholar. Who doesn't respect the "rags to riches" phenomenon that brings admiration to those who choose to educate themselves and who put honor and country before wealth? Such was the character of this humble man from Springfield, Illinois.

Many years ago I had the opportunity to move into another veterinary position when the one I had been working at vanished. It entailed driving to another part of the state, to find a place to live as well as obtain some furniture and a new wardrobe of sorts. The practice at which I arrived had just lost, indefinitely, the owner who had a near-fatal heart attack. I was a single man at the time and so uprooting a family and all that goes with it was not an issue with me. It was a wonderful opportunity to see another part of the state and, being single, a chance to explore, in my spare time, the many little villages that comprise over fifty percent of the state's rural population. Southern New York State, usually referred to as the southern tier, harbors many such little villages, each with unique "personality," be it a women's museum, a baseball hall of fame, and even several villages that pride themselves on the unusual antiques they proudly display to sell to a public willing to part with their funds.

Now, Mr. Abraham Lincoln was not a particularly handsome man. He was tall but not muscular, and according to some records he had reached the height of six feet-four inches at the age of twenty-one. I had read that as an adult he is believed to have a disease known as Marfan's Syndrome, although never verified. He and his family twice suffered the ravages of malaria. He was running for election for the presidency of the United States when something that is not particularly well known evidently greatly improved his chances of election.

Lincoln Bedell statue, Westfield, New York

A young lady in western New York State came upon Mr. Lincoln's picture one day. Her name: Gracie Bedell, age eleven years. Miss Bedell was one of eleven children, one having died prior to her birth and two after. Her father, Norman, had just returned home with a picture of Mr. Lincoln. The entire family was very politically active and Mr. Bedell was a strong abolitionist. Heated discussions often pervaded the entire family as well as their local church. When, upon seeing Mr. Lincoln's picture this child had very definitive thoughts about the man. So, on October 15th, 1860 she sent a letter to Mr. Lincoln letting him know exactly how she felt. Her entire family would vote for him she said, but she wanted the whole country to vote for him. She wanted him to be our next president and in the letter she told him that he looked very sad and if he had a beard he would greatly improve his chances for election. She said that she, and especially the ladies, loved to see men with beards– thought them to be distinguished. Mr. Lincoln wrote back to Gracie, wondered if he would look rather silly with whiskers but thanked her for the letter. He started to grow whiskers shortly after.

Now, as we all know, Abraham Lincoln became our next President and all the while that he was campaigning he sported a beard. After his winning the election on his inaugural trip to the White House Mr. Lincoln's train made the circuitous route from Springfield, Illinois eastward and stopped in Westfield, New York. When the crowd gathered he asked for a little girl by name of Gracie Bedell. A little boy pointed her out. She went up to the new President whereas he picked her up, kissed her, thanked her and told her he was growing the beard just for her. He was the only President in all history at that time to have a beard. And he died with his beard intact; proof one more time that the course of history can be altered at times by seemingly inconsequential acts. Thank you, Gracie Bedell!

* * * * * * *

Barnyard Full Of Animals

Almost seventy years ago, a gentleman by the name of Dan West, a dairy farmer in Indiana, returned from Spain, tired and haggard from seeing the fighting in the Spanish Civil War. He was a volunteer relief worker for the Church of the Brethren. He pondered over the ugly fate that such violence can wreak upon the populace, the unfortunate children and the widows left behind. Yet, after leaving Spain he hungered to do something more, perhaps to placate his conscience, perhaps to calm his aching heart over what he had experienced while overseas. And yet he had found himself totally helpless since no shipments of food, clothing or other staples had been permitted at the time to be sent abroad to the people of this ravaged country.

As a well-known dairyman in his community he organized a group of fifteen other dairymen and together each contributed one dairy animal to a family of another country: Puerto Rico. The first three animals were named: Faith, Hope and Charity. Thus, established in 1944, this wonderful fledgling organization was named Heifers For Relief. Certain guidelines needed to be drawn up to insure longevity of this new program. First and foremost: The first born female of the donated animals must be given to another needy family. To this day this scenario known as "Passing On the Gift" has been repeated literally thousands of times around the world. Second: The program must be sustainable indefinitely. Third: It must empower women. Fourth; Husbandry methods have to be ecologically sound and will not damage any croplands.

Some years later the name was changed to Heifer Project International and even later to Heifer International. This wonderful organization, based in Little Rock, Arkansas, is funded primarily by private donations and to this day it is well-recognized in schools throughout the country by the clever way in which it solicits funds.

Heifer International has served in over 125 countries and at any given time may be involved in projects in the lush valleys of eastern Kentucky to far away Kenya, and from Thailand to Tunisia. As a worker volunteer, my travels with Heifer International to Vietnam and Thailand, an eighteen day experience, has made me ever the richer in seeing the goodness and the ingenuity of people of struggling nations. Our travelling group, including four of us who were veterinary practitioners, had several personally rewarding experiences; in one village we vaccinated a small herd of young animals against two diseases prevalent there. We also surgically neutered two young male bovines at the request of the families in that same little village. Their graciousness and gratefulness was immeasurable!

Over fourteen million families have been assisted in raising their standards of living from abject poverty to a semblance of relative wealth. At any given time there are literally hundreds of projects being served throughout the world. Additionally, Heifer has partnered with countries such as Germany in administering a program in the Golden Triangle of Burma, Laos and Thailand. The goal is to reduce the production of poppies, a source of heroin, by substituting other profitable crops. In Albania Heifer International started a "guns-for-cows" exchange program. And in Romania it is working with Rotary Club to end the serious hunger situation there. Presently some 30 species of animals are involved in the program, from cattle to camels, from silkworms to goats and from llamas to honeybees.

Heifer International receives ninety-seven per cent of its funds from private companies and individuals. More than 1000 church congregations in the United States support Heifer International. Additionally, it has a 501(c)3 status. The Bill and Melinda Gates Foundation has contributed approximately $50 million to Heifer International. And to top it off, Forbes Magazine lists Heifer as one of its top ten charities. And all of this, a grass roots program started by a humble benevolent farmer in Indiana, shows very poignantly how "From a tiny acorn a mighty Oak may grow."

* * * * * * *

GRANDPA

I was 10 years old then and I remember Grandpa sitting in his usual place next to the stove in my Grandma's half of the old farmhouse. I'll never forget that scene–Grandma washing the supper dishes and Grandpa just sitting there–most of the time with his very long, gnarled walking stick held in his equally gnarled hand, next to the oil cloth-covered kitchen table. And he loved chewing his Beechnut tobacco, rolling the wad in the rounded cheeks that filled most of his red-veined face. He sported a heavy gray bushy mustache that frequently was streaked with tobacco juice. The ever-present spittoon, always too far away for him to reach, became a fixture for him to master–usually unsuccessfully. Grandma, of course, got stuck mopping up the floor

We laughed good-naturedly when he threatened us, which was frequently, for whatever infraction he could conjure up. And if we were nearby when he made his trip to the outhouse we would taunt him playfully just to see how good his aim was with his infamous stick that became his trademark whenever he ventured from the house.

Grandpa Lucas and his two sons, Emil and Albert ran the dairy farm with a tight fist when the Depression made them totally rely for sustenance on meat from poultry, pigs and dairy animals that no longer produced, as well as fruits and vegetables from the farm. These solid German immigrants had to make a go of it since Medicaid and food stamps had not yet existed. My father had developed a keen interest in honeybees and with up to 3000 pounds of honey to sell at the farmers' market every year he was reasonably assured that his six children would not only grow but flourish. And we all learned how to work, all six of us. Did we ever! From picking up freshly dug up potatoes and putting them into bushel baskets and loading them onto the truck, to the daily, smelly drudgery of cleaning the cow barn.

We had 3000 laying Leghorn hens as well as every named potato imaginable… well over 1000 bushels for eating and peddling to "those city folks." We supplied the Saratoga Raceway with that sparkling white rye straw that the horse-men so craved for their prized horses and we sold the grain to the bakeries in Albany.

But no matter what we did or where we did it, Grandpa was always there or nearby. If not chewing his tobacco he would be smoking his stubby cigar. At strawberry picking time he would carefully pack the juicy strawberries into crates to be taken to market. If we tried to snitch even one berry his swift porky hand would beat us to the draw.

And one day, the urge to try a smoke got the better of me as I eyed the remaining stub of the cigar he had just tossed away. Stealthily, I walked toward my bicycle, lit the remaining stub and headed home from the field. I had no idea that cigars are not to be inhaled. Nausea and dizziness took its toll in a few minutes as I rounded the bend of the lane to our house. I remember little else except a brief sojourn under our lilac bush where I felt like I was dying and wished at the moment that I could. Grandpa was the first to know of my transgressions and when my mother heard of it I looked askance and saw the smug look on his face. There may even have been a knowing smile–a rarity for this curmudgeon of a man. I had gotten my come-uppance.

Then on June 9th 1946, a Sunday, this hulk of a man suddenly died. Dropsy, they called it–a name now referring to congestive heart failure. At age eighty-one he had been the patriarch of this struggling immigrant family. His death marked the end of an era. Bittersweet memories often make me reflect on the quiet, stalwart ways of this hardworking family–*my family*–so eager to make their way in America, their new home.

* * * * * * *

Familiarity

Roland and Gertie were immigrants from southern Germany; For many years they had lived near the border with Switzerland before emigrating to the United States. They'd recall hearing the immigration officer at the bridge, when going over into Switzerland, whistling his favorite tunes almost every day, and usually off-key. The station also employed a veterinarian who had to check animals for signs of scabies as well as making sure all papers were in order. It was well known that the immigration officer and the veterinarian often played cards when business was slow at that little station.

It was heated in winter by an old-fashioned pot belly stove. On occasion only the veterinarian or the immigration officer was visible in the little building and rumor was that the two took turns napping. Roland knew the immigration officer, Hans, as a kindly man, seldom given to harsh warnings about crossing over the border when all the papers were not exactly as they should be. But occasionally he'd have a bad day, ranting at tourists unfamiliar with policy and sternly sending them back to fetch additional papers.

Hans was always eating something, a sandwich or an apple whenever they encountered him on their crossing to see their dear friends in Germany's sister city. He was a portly fellow, his belt never visible around his huge girth. His belly would jiggle as he walked back and forth at his station, sometimes just for lack of anything better to do. Odds are that he played a robust Santa Claus when the Christmas season came around. He even sported the metal rimmed glasses so commonly appearing on Mr. Claus whenever his likeness appeared in magazines.

When Gertie had Emil and his frau, Bertha over for a holiday dinner Emil was pleasantly surprised by her wonderful generosity. He loved the baked turnips and the sauerbraten that she so easily turned out. It never occurred to him that Bertha herself could, if she had a mind to, bake the very same dish... maybe even add a little more spice to suit his taste. But she seemed to lack that creativity, despite knowing full well that Emil devoured almost everything she cooked up anyway.

They had a lovely time over the tasty food, and the light-hearted conversation. When the evening drew to a close, Gertie again outdid herself and gave the visiting couple a generous helping of sauerbraten to take home. And Roland had gone out to the garden and returned with an armful of freshly pulled turnips. For Emil it was as though Christmas had come early. He was a happy man.

When it came time to leave the couple said their good-byes and straddled their bicycles to cross over the river to their beloved homeland. Slowing down a bit at the duty gate he heard the man who replaced Hans for that shift shouting for them to stop. "What for!" yelled Emil, never thinking that he too was now technically a foreigner entering another country. Annoyed over the audacity of such a stranger daring to order this huge man and his wife to accountability the couple merely continued on.

It was very late that evening when the bell at the door rang loudly and continuously. Emil and Bertha had already retired. In his night clothes he hurriedly dragged himself to the front door, wishing that the incessant ringing would stop and not awaken his wife who was already asleep. Upon opening the door an immigration officer confronted Emil: "You must come viz me," he said. "Ve have been following you and you haf broken za rules of our country and I haf been ordered to take you in. Also, you haf taken 'zis vegetables, za turnips, visout za proper paper."

Obviously Emil hadn't realized that the immigration officer was a new replacement from another station and he had also totally forgotten that produce was not allowed across the border. Another might have recognized him and looked the other way. After being fully awakened and his faux pas explained Emil was properly reprimanded and exonerated of his misdeed. He quietly crept up the stairs with a sense of embarrassment, and a resolve to be more aware of the law. Unfortunately, the turnips had to go back to Germany.

* * * * * * *

BEES, BEES: HOLY SMOKE!

My Dad, a dairy farmer, was the consummate beekeeper. It always appeared to us kids that he was in his total heaven working the occasional Sunday afternoon in his various bee yards in the area's farming community. Of course, farmers were happy to have well-managed honeybees on their property for they were responsible for pollinating the apple or pear orchards on their farms. At times my father had a total of up to 150 colonies of honey bees in the local orchards. When Spring came he'd placed his order for bees and they would arrive at the train station in neat little screened boxes with the queen bee tucked safely into her own smaller screen box within the larger one. Father would pay us a nickel each to hammer together the wooden frames with the wax membrane secured within their borders. They would be the foundation for these ingenious little critters to build their store of honey for the future. Their hives are their pantry for the daily food supply and in all reality also their IRA, with "no penalty for early withdrawal!"

It is claimed by some that bee venom has great value in the fight against arthritis and my father firmly believed in that theory. He knew almost intuitively how to manage bees. It was rare that he was stung, for he knew, possibly through the experience of years at this craft, that bees keenly sense the attitude of the bee handler. They can smell anxiety, anger, and how the handler treats them. If he was occasionally stung he would gently pick the insect up by its wings and remove it without fanfare.

Killing a honeybee causes a familiar sweet scent to be released which triggers others to take action since it disturbs their sense of quietude immediately. Additionally, colors, odors, vibrations, weather, time of day and seasons all play a part in the behavior of honeybees.

When Fall came it was time to take the honey from these unsuspecting workers, but leaving enough in their pantry for them to survive the long winters of the East coast. They had very little to say about the matter. They would angrily leave the hive and circle around our veiled heads protesting such a larcenous act with the most audible and angry buzzing. Only a few well directed puffs of smoke by one of us would tend to settle them down. Smoking them with smoldering burlap is a well-recognized and accepted way of calming down irate hives of honeybees.

In a good year it was not unusual to take frames of honey from the hive, each weighing upward of twenty pounds and to extract or separate the honey from the hexagon-shaped cells so beautifully constructed by these master craftsmen. Our entire family was involved in this venture. After using a steam knife to melt the wax covering over the cells of honey we would, by way of an extractor, spin out, with centrifugal force, the amber liquid within. One year, in the late 1940's we had over 3000 pounds of clover honey to take to market, most of it put up in five pound pails. Father even had some customers in New

York City to whom he shipped what he referred to as his liquid gold.

Insects are the largest of all families in the animal kingdom. And bees are part of that family. There are known to be over ten thousand types of bees. Yellow jackets, with which we are all familiar, are actually not part of the bee family. Rather, they are part of a different group known as wasps.

The intelligence of bees has long been underestimated. The worker bees, the drones, the forager bees and the queen bee all comprise part of a bee colony. When a source of nectar is found the direction in which fellow bees are guided to that source is well documented. Each bee is given a minuscule taste of the procured nectar and then in a very intricate dance done by the worker bee, the others are directed to that source. So intricate is that dance performance that it has been shown that, since the sun moves one degree to the West every four minutes a calculation is made by the dancing bee to allow for that movement and then adjust the flight pattern accordingly. Even the distance to that source of nectar is calibrated and noted in the lead bee's guidance system. Who would ever imagine that these little creatures are endowed with such unbelievable intelligence?

It is more than a little ironic that many years later I, as a veterinarian, was called to a farm on a Sunday afternoon to examine a small Jersey cow that was lying in a shallow creek. Farmers love to let their cattle roam in their orchards. It can be difficult to keep weeds and overgrowth from around the trees with a cutting mower but cattle can easily keep brush and weeds under control. As it turns out the cow got too close to a bee hive and was stung around the face; apparently she panicked and butted her head onto the hive tipping it over. That apparently unleashed the angry bee colony to the point of self-defense; running wildly through the bee yard she tipped over still another hive of bees. Blinded by her swollen eyes and face she attempted to cross a stream bed and fell. While not drowning, she lay there for over two hours and the toxins of the stings caused massive swelling around the poor wretch's face, neck and front quarters. Fortunately, the farmer, a family friend, called in desperation and in fear of losing the animal. Thankfully, when I arrived the bees retreated and I was able to inject intravenous fluids, and a steroid as well as an antihistamine intramuscularly. I stayed in attendance for almost an hour, left on a quick errand to another nearby farm and then returned to witness a rather dramatic improvement in the animal's condition. She recovered uneventfully overnight.

My brother reflects nostalgically on those years when we were youngsters. He still manages to take care of a hive or two of honeybees and, if lucky, probably reaps just enough honey for the occasional stack of pancakes. I, on the other hand, prefer to be as far away from them as I can be regardless of how intelligent they are! Thank God we don't all love the same things!

* * * * * *

BUFFALO, CITY OF GOOD NEIGHBORS, AND SNOW

The newspaper that morning headlined the accumulation of snow in much of western New York but especially in Buffalo. As a transplant to that part of New York State it never dawned on me that this venerable city and historic area was the brunt of good-natured jokes regarding its reputation of, not only being a "city of good neighbors," but also more humorously as "the snow capital of the East." What is often referred to as "lake-effect weather," western New York State receives more than its share of the white stuff almost without fail every winter. When the Great Lakes finally freeze over, if they indeed do, the weather essentially settles down to a normal cold, snowy and overcast picture.

The Blizzard of '77 is well-documented in the annals of western New York history. If one were to mention that very term during discussions of snowy climates it would immediately evoke a dramatic response. Work at that time essentially came to a complete halt during as well as on several days following that blizzard. There were cars abandoned on many highways. It was not unusual to see people take to skis and sleds to commute to the local deli or post office or to merely check on their neighbors. Several deaths were recorded. And people really got to know one another, sometimes a neighbor in need of groceries, or for a jump start for his car–even if there was no place to go with it, considering the roads were basically obliterated by a vast sea of snow, often two or three feet in depth. Such emergencies tend to bring out the very best in people, and sometimes the worst.

As a relative newcomer to that part of New York and as a new owner of an animal hospital, it was my luck to experience the vagaries of a climate that caught me, as a newcomer, by complete surprise, good or bad. It all started on that fateful day with a power outage in mid-afternoon. We had just heard the radio report and forecast for that night and the next day as well and, expecting the worst I dismissed all of my employees allowing them to be at home with their children who were also dismissed from school early in anticipation of the blizzard.

I was now alone in the building. There was housekeeping to be done in that the animals had to have their cages cleaned again and they needed to be fed. My major concern was the power outage. No one knew how long that would last, maybe only a few hours, maybe a day, maybe two or even three days. No one knew what to expect. We had several animals in residence there, four cats, and seven dogs, some having just undergone surgery, some due for surgery the next day. And all the dogs were yelping for attention. Maybe they were frightened over the lack of light in the room and the foreboding black skies at that moment. I could feel their very anxiety but felt rather helpless to calm them down. The telephone lines were, thankfully, still working and I called my wife. I anticipated the worst. But she was in full control except for a demolished storm door with its shattered glass. How lucky I was to have a solid, in-control mate "to hold down the fort" at home, several miles away. And the three kids were having the time of their lives.

Meanwhile, I gathered the gorgeous ferns from the reception room and hung them in the kennel room which was being heated by boiling water in a large steel cooker. It was cozy and toasty warm there and the animals seemed to accept their fate as I shone the flashlight into the compartments to check each one over one more time. Moments later the telephone rang and my wife was wanting to know when I would be home for dinner. There was silence on my part. I feared her being alone and at the same time wanting to be certain all would be well at the animal hospital with my new task of pet overseer for the night. I would make-do with some soup and snacks. Fortunately, I had several large blankets that pet owners had left when bringing in injured animals. They would serve as a source of warmth while I anticipated getting at least a little sleep for the next twelve hours on those cold vinyl benches in the reception area.

Early the next morning, at perhaps seven, an employee of the power company stopped by to see how we were doing. "You okay?" asked the lineman. "We're pretty much cleaned up now." One doesn't usually expect that kind of inquiry. I felt a new warmth coming over me. But then again, Buffalo is indeed a "City of Good Neighbors" and I was told that by ten a.m. we would again be back in business. And indeed we were. My Buffalo, New York had again made history.

* * * * * * *

Is There A God?

It was a typical late evening and my wife and I were quietly sorting through Scripture readings trying to find appropriate material for our church monthly discussion group. When the phone rang at 9:45 we were a bit nervous to receive a call at that hour. It was a Rabbi from southern Colorado calling to ask if we had a daughter named Kathryn. Our hearts jumped in nervous anticipation of what might follow. Their friends were coming in from Denver and were going along this country road heading due South to their home, to dialogue on their faiths. And here we, a couple in Arizona were also doing the very same thing.

What followed was enough to make our hearts leap with fear. In the dark as they were proceeding South the couple saw papers strewn all over a stretch of road and along with them what appeared to be a wallet. The lady, I shall call her Mary, insisted her husband turn back to examine these items, and maybe discover a clue of sorts. He did so but reluctantly. They were late already for their dinner engagement with their friends. How often would the average motorist be guided by... whatever, curiosity, perhaps even a form of divine inspiration, serendipity, to stop and check out something like this?

It turned out to be our daughter's wallet and its contents containing many, many dollars and all the valuable papers that one often carries on his/her person.

And it further heightened our fears and concerns after the Rabbi passed on to us that there were several prisons in the area. Thoughts of not-so-savory parolees hitchhiking and being picked up by a benevolent traveler crossed our minds immediately.

Our attempts to reach our daughter were futile as the cell phone kept glaring this strange but poignant message: "no reception." We left a message on her cell telling of our concerns and we waited–and waited–seemingly forever.

Within 10 minutes our daughter called, chipper as usual, to say a cheery Hello. She had no idea what was happening–nor did she check her messages. –Serendipity?

Kathryn detected my profound anxiety and concern–could not in any way understand what the trembling in our voices was all about.

And then we asked her:

"Kathryn, where is your wallet?"

And her response: "Oh, My God!"

At least we could breathe a sigh of relief. She was *okay*. The wallet certainly was secondary. She was at the other end of the line and she was safe!

Further inspiration! Mary had quickly picked up everything she could find, including the wallet, the papers, and of course, the extensive assortment of currency. Again, Ironic? A trucker had slowed down, stopped–to avoid an accident and then was about to begin helping himself to some of the "goodies." Mary approached him hurriedly and reminded him that something is not right in this entire picture, and that what she is seeing, while not hers, belongs to someone who is likely in great distress, and that she, Mary, would make a sincere attempt to locate the owner. And, indeed she did!

Our grateful daughter as well as we, her parents, humbly thanked all parties involved. But there is more: Every penny, all the currency, all the papers, and credit cards were recovered. With one exception: It appears that our new telephone acquaintances were apparently not satisfied that they had done their good deed for the day. The husband, who works at a prison, passed the site the next morning and for good measure stopped by to make sure nothing was left behind. He found only one small item... a small brown coin about one inch in diameter. On its surface was something no one could possibly miss... the raised image of an angel.

I said to myself: "There is a GOD!"

* * * * * * *

THE DRIVE IN

Who doesn't remember the drive-in theater? If one were to drive across the country one would be quite lucky to find a drive-in theatre somewhere in the back reaches of small-town U.S.A. They have largely given way to the modern multiplex screens with reclining plush seats, air conditioning and almost infallible technology. Research has shown that for every drive-in theater that is still in operation there are six that are classified as "dead." In fact, there are some 3000 drive-in theaters nationwide that are defunct, or gone, or simply classified officially as "dead." A list is readily available for each and every state in the country.

In our day these drive-ins were anything but "dead." More than one couple has failed to see the ending of a movie! Sometimes, of course, it was because both fell asleep in each other's arms. But then again there were more than a few who simply lost interest in the subjects on the screen and were diverted to other interests. There have been stories of parents not permitting their son or daughter to attend the drive-in in a vehicle that had a back seat and, more preferably also had bucket seats in front with a console in between the two.

We, of course, were not of that ilk. We did things that only kids who pooled their resources could do. We chipped in for gasoline, even in those days when gasoline averaged around thirty-five cents a gallon. It was in the days when sniffer dogs and wary attendants didn't exist! They'd let in a car carrying a couple, maybe two, with no hesitation at all, never realizing that when a parking spot was secured three or four more kids might come tumbling out of the trunk. Unfortunately sometimes only a lowly pickup truck was all that one of us could scrounge up. But we'd sit outside contentedly by the speaker pole and sometimes giggle at the scenes or arbitrate who was supposed to bring the snacks or even who ate the last apple. We had "just plain good old fun."

The last time I attended a drive-in theater was in 1953. The theater was behind a Howard Johnson's restaurant. It was very close to our high school. That night Billy was the only one with a car and we argued over who would be able to go since there were ten of us and no matter how we figured it that car would not hold all of us. He was so very "morally inclined" that he wouldn't even entertain the idea of us sneaking in. We all agreed that we must respect his moral upbringing. It took four rounds of voting to just accomplish that feat alone. Thus, Billy said that the best he could do, considering his upright character, was to drive in by himself and we'd find him somewhere in that vast field of cars and pickup trucks. He'd agreed that he could hang the speaker outside the car window and we'd all sit on the ground chat, and munch our goodies.

Howard Johnson's, officially HoJo today, had a six-foot solid wooden pole fence surrounding the property to discourage the riff-raff from sneaking in. Fair enough we thought, but we'd already committed ourselves to join Billy and it was too late to back out. Tight along the fence were six steel fifty gallon-drums that held all the spent cooking oil from the restaurant. It would likely be taken away by a hauler every two or three weeks. Whoa, we thought, how lucky could we get! One by one we would vault up onto the covered drums and easily pop over the top of the fence. Golly that was so easy; until I came along, the second to last of the bunch. As I bounded up ready to make the final leap over the fence the cover spun over and I slipped feet first into the drum. There had to be almost three feet of oil in there with me in it, sending some of it over the sides and onto the ground. Fred, behind me, was of no help whatsoever. He was so hysterically consumed in laughter that he almost choked to death. Worse, he whistled for the others to come to see this magical feat that I had pulled off. The uproarious symphony of laughter from the guys almost got us thrown out. And, to top it off Billy wouldn't let me ride home in his car; he took Fred home to borrow his dad's truck and I'd have to sit in the back on a bale of hay. I was totally humiliated and vowed I would become more like Billy. I lost not only my pride but a new pair of khaki pants. It was one of the tougher things I had to explain to my aggravated parents. If I had drowned it might have been easier.

* * * * * * *

THE BIG GAME HUNTER

As a young man in college I was invited to a cousin's home for Thanksgiving. It entailed taking a bus and ferry several hundred miles from the University in the upper peninsula of Michigan, to his home in the lower peninsula near Holland, Michigan. After all those benign cafeteria meals in college this was a welcome treat. Upon arriving and being shown around the farm my cousin showed me his collection of guns–big ones, small ones and everything in between.

The day after I arrived we walked through the considerable acreage that they farmed. He was so proud of being a hunter, for sport and for providing meat for the table. I had learned a few things myself about hunting, and especially about the varmints that destroyed our crops at home, making huge mounds of dirt that clogged the machinery and made a general mess of the crop land.

Jimmy was a few years younger than I and soon to be college bound himself. He kept track of his kill: Twelve woodchucks, dozens of partridges, thirty-seven pheasants and five deer. His dad, a large animal veterinarian and dairy farmer, bought him a newer gun, a double barrel shotgun. Now, if he missed the pheasant the first time he had another shot at him before reloading.

I could never quite understand how a veterinarian could co-exist within himself as both a healer of animals and one who could, with a metal projectile, easily terminate the life of a perfectly healthy animal. His dad had challenged him to beat his record of kills even though he had a head start of many years.

I had just read about the Gatling gun a few weeks earlier. Gatling guns have a revolving barrel that fires 16 bullets, one after another without reloading. Jokingly, I wondered if Jimmy secretly had his eye on one out there somewhere. He could theoretically kill 16 deer if they all lined up politely, and like dominoes they'd all fall in a rhythmic pattern. That would indeed give him a new record. His dad would be proud!

Summer came and I returned home to the farm to help out evenings after my job as laborer on a road construction project. Weekends gave me a slight reprieve and I wanted to test my skills as a hunter. I had great memories of my skill with a B-B gun on shooting tin cans setting on the top of fence posts. And with my dad's 30-30 rifle I could zero in on those woodchucks and thus be the family hero.

That turned into a disaster when, after I had wounded one little animal, he propped himself up as best he could and looked me straight in the eye with a mournful look that I've never forgotten.

Better to stick with a smaller weapon and avoid such confrontations from now on, I thought.

Then, the pheasant season came and this reformed hunter gave it another try. Our farm had a wetland, then referred to as a swamp. It was near our house and it encompassed some five to six acres. It was too wet for the grass to be mowed and so it grew, like elephant grass, some three feet tall. It was a perfect place for pheasants to forage and also a wonderful place for re-al, bona fide pheasant hunters. This next morning would be a perfect start of my great day of renewal.

As I stalked slowly into the grass, I didn't have time to even ready my psyche for this new adventure when a cock pheasant made his presence known a mere eight feet away. The cacophony of language that spewed forth... that usual rau-cous cry of the pheasant took me by such surprise that I was momentarily immobilized... frozen in my tracks, so-to-speak. I did recover soon enough though, and took aim and by then he had already assumed his own flight pattern, no less than thirty feet up. I brought him down with a single shot from the shot-gun–incredible marksman that I was! I had only winged him!

He landed, and instantly disappeared in the thicket of grass with me right behind him. I thought I could easily grab him but that was not to be. He zigged and zagged, always eight to ten feet ahead of me until I finally took the approach that any great hunter, big game or small, would take: I *threw* the gun at the moving grass and stopped him cold in his tracks!

As I retrieved him I almost cried! He was a rainbow of pure iridescence that sparkled so incredibly in the morning sun. How could a living creature be so gorgeous, so very beau-tiful? If he was part of God's plan I had no business to be de-stroying it. And as I carried him to the chopping block I vowed that my hunting days were over, and indeed they were, some 60 years ago.

****

THE SKI BUMS

For twenty-three years a loosely organized group of us fel-
lows skied together at the same ski hill every Tuesday night
from the first decent snowfall until the Winter finally bid us
adieu in late March. We would all meet at about 7:15 p.m. at
the ski lodge. Maybe the impatient ones in the group would
take a run or two and wait for us before mounting the chairlift
for still another run. Then, once a year we'd plan a trip to a distant ski resort, most often out west in Vail or Lake Tahoe. One
year we threw care to the wind, ignored our wives' lamenta-
tions about the cost and planned a trip to Switzerland. Davos,
Switzerland was one of the most gorgeous areas we had skied
in all of our years together.

We had never experienced such beauty or, for that matter,
such cold weather in all of our lives. Klosters, 9.8 miles distant
from Davos was made famous by Prince Charles and Diana.
On one occasion we skied the long trek from Davos to Klosters
where the celebrated couple spent much of their time, most
likely so as to retain a semblance of privacy. We never did see
them there but we were told that Charles was not particularly
adept at the sport and the late Diana was essentially a "tag-
along" on her skis.

The beautiful part of skiing in Switzerland, or all of Europe
for that matter, is that the access to the resorts is so easy by
train. And the trains in Europe are extremely predictable on
their time schedules. Often we would see a youngster or two

standing alongside the tracks, waiting for the train in a small village, backpack strapped on and ready for school. Within a minute or two the train would appear, right on time.

The Swiss take great pride in developing their ski resorts. It is not unusual to see fences rolled up along the ski trail so that the runs are more navigable. On one occasion we skied through the remains of an onion patch next to a tavern. On the side of the tavern was a large steer, tethered the building, likely the "reserved" champion for the banquet planned for the following week.

We had missed the most recent train back to Davos so we imbibed freely at the pub while listening to the bar-keep telling stories about "those crazy Americans." That is, until he found out that we were from New York State. Conversation became a bit more subdued at that point but the laughter continued the entire time we spent there. Laughter, the universal language, knows no boundaries.

We even took a couple of hours to stop in a nearby hospital for animals to say "Hello," introduce ourselves and to learn a few things about veterinary medicine in Switzerland. Many of the procedures performed there in the Switzerland animal hospital are identical to the way we perform ours. Even some of the equipment manufacturers are the same.

Several years prior to our ski venture I had the wonderful opportunity to employ a young lady veterinarian from neighboring Innsbruck, Austria. She was on a temporary visa and was licensed to work in our country for a protracted period of time. She was a delight to be around and had a very patient-oriented manner. But her time with us was abbreviated when her husband's research position ended rather abruptly.

It was merely a "skip and a hop," on skis, of course, to ski almost half the way to St. Moritz. We could board the train in Davos, disembark at a convenient point and literally ski into the village of St. Moritz. There, it seems is another world to be sure. The glitz, the sable coats and mink apre-ski boots and other attire attest to a world totally foreign to us ski bums. We were happily confident that ours was the world we most wanted to be in. That remains to this day.

Since then, moving to Arizona over 16 years ago, the trips to Heavenly Ski Resort, Steamboat Springs and other western ski areas have been a new experience altogether. Friendships are so very different now–the camaraderie is not the same and the skiing, while superb lacks an indefinable quality.

No more "saluting the slopes" after the last run with a nip of Southern Comfort to attest to a night of fun and friendship until another Tuesday night rolls around. The love and warmth engendered in our over-twenty year friendships is still a deep part of each of us. We live it nostalgically and still embrace it fully. And if not on the ski slopes then most likely on our summer patio get-togethers for beer and brats and to fully enjoy one another's company. True friendship also has no boundaries.

* * * * * * *

ONE IN, ONE OUT!

Drugs in our society are here to stay and the world knows it. I am referring to illegal drugs–drugs that stimulate, hypnotize, sedate, cause euphoria, eliminate pain, and generally cause an unreal existence on a daily basis. Sadly, there are people all over our society who are so addicted that some, or all of their normal reasoning capacity seems to have been destroyed.

One such individual was determined to get a fix on a drug that we in the veterinary profession utilize rather extensively. This drug shall not be named herein for obvious reasons because it sets up a reasonable probability that someone reading this may get ideas.

My telephone suddenly awakened me at 2:00 a.m. on a weekday several years ago. It was the local police department calling from my animal hospital parking lot. They wanted me to know of a burglary there and to also come in and possibly identify a suspect. Someone had set off the security alarm and one of our friends, a client who lived directly across the street, upon hearing the alarm wisely called the police department. The police arrived and saw a white car parked diagonally in the middle of our otherwise vacant parking lot. Ironically, there was a full moon out, clearly defining this vehicle. But no one was to be seen anywhere near the car so the police assumed there was a burglary in progress. Calling in other backup they moved in and upon distant observation they saw the mode of entry–a broken double-pane glass front door. They knew immediately that the individual was inside by the inward-facing of the broken glass in the door. Choosing to not make further needless and risky advances, they waited outside and within ten to twelve minutes the person appeared, staggering and seemingly intoxicated. He had found no drugs. They were safe under double lock and key. Unfortunately, he did find a number of small syringes that he carried out carefully, in both hands. He was arrested and faced prosecution for burglary and larceny. He was well known in the immediate neighborhood as a drug junkie with several previous arrest records. I counted my blessings in that no vandalism was done and the valuable instruments on the premises were still inside and undamaged.

Actually, it was prior to this that there was the case of Brutus, who might well have been named Houdini for the incredible stunt he pulled off. He was so comically bazaar-looking in his appearance that one might easily laugh upon first seeing him. His right ear hung down while his left ear was erect. And his right lower lip was drooping so that one could see his lower teeth, but on the right side only. He had been injured in the face several years ago and the resultant nerve damage left poor Brutus' face partially paralyzed. He was brought in to the hospital the previous day for a gash on his right rear leg. After admitting him I felt it prudent to keep him overnight after surgery to make certain that his stitches remained intact.

What happened from there on still remains a partial mystery. Brutus apparently felt he needed to go home. He wanted desperately to be home; he had no desire to stay at my animal hospital any longer than absolutely necessary. Like Houdini, Brutus did a disappearing act. A quick inspection done first thing in the morning verified that he was *not* in the animal hospital–anywhere! Alarmed and chagrined, both at the same time, we immediately called the owner and explained the situation.

"Oh," said the owner. "Brutus is sitting on the front porch. I paid no attention to his being there until just this very minute when I realized he wasn't supposed to be there. He was supposed to be with you guys!"

How very, very embarrassing to us. It may well have ended quite differently.

We spent part of that day going through all the sequences that this determined dog went through to escape. First he had to climb over a six-foot chain link fence and gate and drop to the other side. Then he needed to push open a heavy, solid-core wooden door to get into the main part of the hospital. Next he had to wander toward the front, in the dark, of course, where he encountered one more solid-core wooden door. And finally he had to turn the door knob of the steel door leading to the outside. This must have taken many, many tries until, alas, he succeeded.

It was then, three months after moving into the new building that Brutus so aptly convinced me that we needed a burglar alarm–not only to keep burglars out but also to keep big, clever dogs in! Thank you, Brutus!

* * * * * * *

CARS GALORE

I tried to count the number of cars our family had since marriage and I seemed to lose track every time. At first count it was eleven; then someone did a recount and it turned out to be thirteen. Either way every car we owned had its own temperament, its way of giving us pleasure or maybe just aggravation. With two daughters now into driving it was always anticipated to have one or the other come home with a story to tell about it, or more likely: "That car is driving me nuts!"

In one incident, while I was stopped at a traffic signal a car ran into the side of mine–minus a driver! The owner of the car, after filling it up with gas went inside to pay the bill, only to return to find his car gone from the pump.

Meanwhile, I was sitting in the traffic line waiting for him to complete his transaction and to come out. My car was the victim of "run and hit." His vehicle sat at the curb against mine and, dumbfounded, he had to walk down, and own up to the damage his car inflicted on mine. That little yellow car caused us a lot of aggravation for a couple of years.

But the weirdest experience our family had, specifically, my son, was when he "lost" his VW Scirocco. It literally disappeared from the apron of the driveway where he always backed it into when coming home from work. How he loved that sporty little vehicle! His life seemed to be identified by it–by how great the sound system was or how he could leave others "in the dust" when the light turned green while on his way home from work.

Anyway, no more than an hour after he parked it in the driveway it vanished. When he went out, scratching his head he had to do some detective work. No Sherlock Holmes or Columbo, he finally did manage to see some tire tracks on the grass behind the car. Weird? He followed them to the edge of the embankment by the driveway, scratched his head some more and then, 100 or so feet toward the bushes he saw one headlight. The rest of the car was entirely hidden in the heavy thicket of the neighbor's field. No living person could have ever hidden that car more thoroughly!

And now he had to retrieve it. Embarrassing as it was he had to ask the neighbor if he could drive it across the tennis court in his backyard and onto the street to take it back home again. The neighbor had that puzzled look on his face but didn't dare ask how that car got there in the first place. Very nonchalantly he gave his consent. The poor kid had "egg on his face" because, regardless of what he might have admitted, Jack, our kindly neighbor, consented. He had that half-smile on his face and just walked into the house.

Then, even worse, there was the Sunday our girls came home from church, parked the car outside of the garage and came in. Ten minutes later the car alarm went off. We were confused; the girls were both inside our home and no one was out by the car. Upon opening the garage door I was horrified to see flames shooting up inside the car by the steering wheel. I kept my wits about me long enough to grab a fire extinguisher, rush out, open the driver's side door and empty the contents of the extinguisher onto the flames. My wife had already called the fire department and within 10 minutes they were there. I had already put the fire out.

Of course, being schooled to do their job thoroughly they trained their four-inch hose onto the entire insides of the car.

The interior was a totally-melted mess, steering wheel, dashboard, seats and all the wiring. Then, in my presence a firemen called in the arson squad. Why? We found out later that the car had previously been in an accident and had not been repaired properly. The roof apparently had a leak near the sunroof and to prevent future drivers from getting wet feet the mechanics stuffed rags under the dashboard. That had set up a perfect place for spontaneous combustion.

The girls had gotten home just in time!

The insurance company wouldn't total the car and sadly we spent months waiting for its repair. It was never the same after that. It developed a mind of its very own. When one turned the directional for a left turn the interior lights came on and when one made a right turn the horn would blow. Finally, in despair, we traded it in for a pickup truck.

* * * * * * *

LUCKY ME

We lived in a small village, population 3200, in Western New York State and it had all the characteristics of many small villages nationwide; a couple of gas stations, a restaurant, a bank, an insurance agency, a barbershop, a dentist, two doctors and of course, a funeral home. The pace was always the same... essentially sleepy, and when the weather changed everyone had something to talk about again. After a few days it settled back to its drowsiness.

One day a cattle truck came through town and stopped by Barney's gas station for a fill-up. You could smell it from 4 blocks away–that characteristic odor that most of us recognized immediately.

Barney's was also the local hangout–the place where the news got to before it was on the local radio station, the restaurant or in the local newspaper. It was rather neat in its own way because you could count on the stories heard there to be essentially correct, maybe with one or two embellishments that perhaps qualified as gossip.

I had been up for many hours the previous night when one of Frank Miller's ewes was giving birth and he needed me there right away, if not sooner! His three hour effort was futile in dislodging the little critters from their warm cubicle. Surely triplets were well worth my sleep time and he made that known, especially after I extracted the last of the three, all alive and squirming.

Now, that day was one of those rare days of a light farm schedule and I could use a little R and R to rejuvenate my spirits. Besides, with 3 youngsters at home, two still in diapers, my nerves were a little frazzled.

My wife bade me adieu and I headed out to the cabin that I was building. While I was working in the crawl space of the cabin I came close to being electrocuted while standing in eight inches of water. I had put a metal staple through a 300 Amp wire that was to electrify my new hot water heater. A huge ball of fire shot out and, dazed, I dropped my staple gun and quickly exited the crawl space as fast as I could. I lay on the floor gasping, wondering if I was still alive or perhaps waiting for an angel to give me some final advice! Fortunately, I had on my new rubber boots which saved my life.

When I arrived home my wife looked at me and said: "Are you alright?" Why would she ask such a silly question? She had heard that the bull in the cattle truck escaped and charged down Main Street. He was evidently very happy to escape such confinement and made it known rather instantly. When one observes bull-riding at rodeos it compared favorably to this galloping mass of muscle and bone. And he was *not* about to be subdued. You could see him occasionally stop, snort and charge at any moving object, once even at an innocent kitty as he flew with clear intent through backyards. Flower and vegetable gardens alike fell victim to the charge of this raging tornado. The village police were dumbfounded as to how to lasso him so they stopped by to see if we had a tranquilizer gun that they could use to bring him down. Ultimately, they and a couple of neighborhood men cornered him as he gave in to his exhaustion and the drama ended there.

My wife instinctively had visions of me impaled on the horns of this 2000 pound, four-legged moving projectile. She had no idea what the reason was that I was as pale as a ghost. When I told her about my close call with death and the 300 Amps of electricity she said: "Thank God, I thought maybe you tangled with that bull."

* * * * * * *

THE HONEY WAGON CREW

Oh, those college days! It seems as though we defined ourselves in our college days by our socio-economic "status." Even
then there were the "have's" and the "have not's." Those of us
lucky enough to be in the latter group had the most fun.

We worked and lived in the riding stables at the University. There were seven of us guys and... no women. Most of us
had experience with horses or at least with scratching out our
existence and at the same time pursuing an education.

Sometimes it was a balancing act to be sure. We'd either be
late to get out of bed to muck out the horse stalls or go to a
class first and run back to the stables and hope our "boss man,"
Frank, a retired army sergeant, hadn't yet come to ride herd on
us. If we slept in late on a weekend when someone else was on
duty he'd come right into our bedrooms and tip our beds
over... with us in them! It was his way to just re affirm his te
nacity as the tough drill sergeant of bygone days.

"Hey, whatsa matter wid ya, ya sick?" he'd say. Frank was
by all measures a tough guy. He'd be chonking on his ever-
present cigar and issuing orders, both at the same time. He was
never satisfied how we loaded the "honey wagon" or how the
horses were fed or bedded.

And yet we all mused over the twinkle in his eye when he
was satisfied that he had riled us up enough. Then he'd proceed
to laugh and walk away. Frank was infuriating and at the same
time lovable in a bizarre sort of way because we all accepted

him. Here was a man who had served his country well, in the Army, and carried some of the inevitable scars of war, both physically and mentally.

We would always invite him, old as he was, to our raucous weekend parties. He'd show up with his cute wife, Sally, a woman some 35 years his junior. He would go on and on and brag about how we weren't men enough to court such a lovely lady.

She had the most seductive way of asking: "Hello, how are you?" The question dripped of sensuousness. We often wondered about Sally's intentions on the days when Frank was away with his cronies at horse shows in another state. Our hormones were alive and well!

The riding stables were at the edge of campus and it seemed that no one had firm jurisdiction over our safety and well-being, neither the campus police or the city police. That was a great advantage for us because we sometimes ended our parties in the wee hours and no one was the wiser. No one really seemed to care.

There were two residences. One, over the tack room, housed four veterinary students and the other, a bit more deluxe, had a huge fireplace. We'd fight over that apartment because we all wanted to have a real fireplace. Unfortunately, though, that residence was butted up against the riding arena and trying to study with thundering hoofs on the other side of the glass was a real challenge.

There were usually fifty-two horses; about one third of those were polo ponies. They were owned by the University; about seventeen or so were owned by students that did *not* have to shovel horse manure into the honey wagon. And, about a third were ponies that were owned by a wealthy horse farmer in the vicinity. They were lent to the University each school year for a token fee.

The years passed, we veterinary students all graduated and we parted company to go on to our careers, seemingly to never see one another again. However, some forty years later I did meet with one roommate, though not a vet student at the time, at the Lawrence Livermore Laboratory in California. Other than that we have only fond memories of that little rustic "equestrian island" on the edge of campus.

Several years ago, however, my wife and I drove back to Ithaca, New York for nostalgic reasons. We wanted to again see the beautiful campus as well as the familiar riding stable complex.

Disbanded, completely leveled–the horse stables, the residences, the hay barns, and the huge arena were all gone! They were replaced by... of all things: a cyclotron with its inanimate metal support structure. How totally unromantic and bland. Neither of us could believe our eyes! How could they do that to us veteran horse care-givers? We were saddened and incredulous beyond belief.

Never again would young students have the experience of working there as a team like we did; or to be confronted by

Frank, the crusty drill sergeant or to have to fill the honey wagon one more time. Thanks, Lord, for the wonderful memories of working and living there with friends, some of whom are my veterinary colleagues scattered about the country.

****

FEAR OUT IN THE PASTURE

Loren called me out one afternoon right after I had gotten back from a difficult surgical case. One of his prize dairy cows was out in the pasture trying to give birth. He knew right then by the position of the animal that this was not a routine birthing. The animal had seemingly given up on the job. She lay, head down, neck outstretched, with eyes almost closed. Her heart rate was very slow and she was quite cold to the touch. She was, in a word, comatose. Diagnosis: milk fever. This disease is not at all the same as eclampsia in women. It is a disturbance of calcium metabolism in that a significant amount of calcium is diverted to the udder via the milk, causing the circulating calcium to be relatively deficient.

I gobbled down a quick half sandwich, slurped a cup of coffee and invited my wife to accompany me, her first time out to a farm with me since our recent marriage. We still had my older four-door Chevy, and a new vet truck would be the next thing on our to-buy list. Nowadays virtually all large animal practices drive a mobile vet truck with all their many drawers and compartments and are capable of being driven with ease through the rough terrain of fields and pastures. She reminded me that she preferred to stay in the car, at least this time, not having been born into a farming family.

Loren and I had to cross a small stream so we left the car some sixty feet away so he helped me carry my equipment across to the ailing cow. I administered a solution of calcium gluconate intravenously very slowly while keeping tabs on her heart rate with my stethoscope. As expected, she slowly raised her head, looked at both of us as if to say: "What are you guys doing here?" It is truly amazing, almost miraculous to watch the almost minute to minute change in disposition in a dairy cow with milk fever as she is being administered this life saving bottle of calcium gluconate.

Meanwhile, I had forgotten completely about my wife in the car across the stream. I couldn't see the car; it was completely surrounded by Loren's curious herd of Holsteins... literally dozens of them. Bovines are a very curious lot; they explore, they sniff, sometimes switch their tails. And they're harmless, even friendly a majority of the time. It would be rare for a dairy cow to bunt a vehicle as though in protest, as might occur with an angry beef animal.

Regardless of the situation Loren and I extracted the calf, with the mother's help of course. All went well after that; the baby was helped to the mother's head area and she vigorously licked it and cleaned it as all bovines do after a birth. A few moments later she got to her feet unassisted.

Suddenly I heard a blast of the car horn, and then a sustained second one. I don't know how long the herd had been exploring the car's contents in the open trunk as well as my wife! At that instant they immediately scattered as though a bolt of lightning had just hit the ringleader and set it all in motion. After that they got no closer than twenty feet from the vehicle. Upon my approaching the car, my wife opened the door.

She looked frightened to say the least! She managed a weak smile and admitted that she was panicking; she didn't see me and she had no idea what to expect from those curious critters... those bulky, friendly "milk factories" that all the world depends on.

* * * * * * *

CHAUTAUQUA, AN AMERICAN UTOPIA

In the far south-western reaches of New York State sits a small community that has an enviable history. It has existed as a community for one hundred thirty-seven years and represents the arts, history, religion, science, music, theater, and opera. It is known as Chautauqua Institution and for nine delectable weeks every Summer it serves to stretch the human mind like no other place in existence. Its name, Chautauqua, is mispronounced by many, but that word has become part of Webster's lexicon.

When first founded in 1874 by Lewis Miller and John Vincent, it was started as an instruction facility for Sunday school teachers. Tents were pitched and hell-fire and brimstone lectures were the hallmark of its daily messages for several months every Summer. Years later it hosted a platform of learning, composition and reading to enhance the intellect of the American public too poor to attend institutions of higher learning and thus the concept of correspondence courses gained great favor there. To this day Chautauqua Institution boasts the oldest continuous book club in America, known as the Chautauqua Literary and Scientific Circle or simply the CLSC.

Seven Presidents of the United States have visited and lectured at Chautauqua, namely William Howard Taft, Ulysses S. Grant , James Garfield, Theodore Roosevelt, Franklin Delano Roosevelt, William McKinley and more recently Bill Clinton.

The famous speech: "I Hate War" by President Franklin Roosevelt was delivered at Chautauqua's mighty outdoor amphitheater in 1936. Other notable visitors include Thomas Edison, Susan B. Anthony, Amelia Earhart, Jack Kemp, Al Gore, Bob Dole and Arizona's own Sandra Day O'Connor. The latter comes yearly.

Over 70 musicians from around the entire United States perform in the Chautauqua Symphony Orchestra every Summer. The orchestra performs three times weekly in addition to supporting opera and ballet performances. And very interestingly, a husband and wife team in the Phoenix Symphony also perform for the entire nine week Season in Chautauqua. Additionally, there are usually four live theater plays as well as at least two operas.

The Music School Festival Orchestra, some 75 strong, is comprised of students from all over the world. Those 75 are the crème-de la crème of some 2000 applicants and they excel mightily.

And while its lecture platform is extensive–twice daily, five days a week, Chautauqua thrives with its emphasis on spiritual nourishment. Almost every religion boasts a denominational house on the grounds and there are morning sermons daily to start off the day.

Sitting on beautiful Chautauqua Lake it also provides a perfect setting for swimmers, boaters and fisherman. Sailing regattas are commonplace and are held by young and old alike.

In 1985 Chautauqua hosted the first Soviet American Conference on Peace. One hundred ten Soviets, from all walks of life converged on those hallowed grounds to experience a taste of American life as well as to hear public discussions by various speakers on the issues involving crime, culture, occupations, education as well as a taste of American music, from the classics to Rock. They were average Russians, far removed from the corridors of the elite, and no doubt sponsored by the Soviet government. The success and the enthusiasm generated at that conference became a major stepping stone for future Soviet American dialogue; one, a year later in Riga, Latvia and one at a later time in Iceland. It was mentioned subsequently in both the New York Times and the US News and World Report.

For the children accompanying their parents there is summer school, mixing play time and classroom study for the entire Season. For that reason auto traffic on the grounds is severely limited for safety reasons. Approximately 150,000 people are there for all or part of the nine week Season. It is both amusing and very rewarding to see children playing Hop-Scotch in the streets or to see huge chalk drawings of various colors gracing the pavement. No other place appears as safe as this wonderful paradise in western New York. It is no wonder that some families have been experiencing Chautauqua for seven and eight generations, some for eighty to ninety years. And it is "home" for us for as long as practical for the coming years.

* * * * * * *

JAMES HERRIOT: RE-VISITED

It was 10:15 on a cold January night. The telephone woke me from an early half-sleep on the couch. As the new owner of a busy country veterinary practice I was ready to slip on my new boots and get out in the field, even at this hour. As an experienced practitioner, I rather relished the challenge of obstetrics and the intrigue and satisfaction of safely delivering a live calf. I also needed to get the job done and get back home to a comfy bed. On the way out I ignored the slightly nagging feeling that maybe I had forgotten something. Anyway, I was in a rush to head out. This cow probably had been kept waiting long enough already and I had a ways to drive. The steady rain of the past two days was settling into a sleet as the mercury dropped below freezing again. My car had a veneer of ice on it, and soon the roads were glazed treachery. One hour and seventeen miles later I slogged through the barnyard to Tony Ransom's cow barn to see the waiting, comatose patient–a 1400 pound Holstein cow.

As soon as I saw Tony he offered: "Yep, I been workin' on her since one o'clock this afternoon without no luck at all, so I figured I might s'well give ya a crack at her, Doc. I just couldn't get that dang calf outta her."

I proceeded to the patient who long ago had given up the struggle to relieve herself of this monstrous burden within. She lay half-in, half-out of the box stall with its twelve-inch concrete sill. About all she could do was let out a low-grade, painful moan as I inserted my lubricated rubber-sleeved arm deep into her pelvic cavity to make an exploratory survey. I knew right then that I was going to be there for awhile. Thoughts of slipping back into a warm bed vanished as fast as the warm rain of yesterday. The head of the calf was twisted grotesquely forward, but the legs were pointing directly toward me.

Normally, the head comes along with the forelegs in the more natural pattern of delivery. Everything was completely dried out; she had no more natural lubricants there to help ease the newborn out of the birth canal. After almost twelve hours of struggling this was the unfortunate result! I hurriedly administered a calcium gluconate solution intravenously to the fading patient and waited–and waited. Usually a dramatic change occurs in the comatose patient within minutes.

No veterinarian in a country practice marvels more or is more genuinely gratified than to see a cow with milk fever come to life so magically. One can sense that wondrous power flowing through the needle into a dying patient. And, indeed, it truly is a miraculous thing.

I continued with my effort to extract that long-dead calf, but every effort seemed to propel me backward instead of forward. Sadly, I could not shake the shadow of my sarcastic client hovering over me with his ever-present barrage of wisdom on how to get my job done better. It only furthered my resolve to not get more frustrated than I already was.

What I needed now was a mechanical hip sling to raise the cow's rear parts to give me more room internally to maneuver the calf. That meant a return trip home to fetch the instrument. It dawned on me now what I had forgotten. My mind seemed clearer now at one-twenty in the morning than it did when I was rousted from my cozy slumber by that annoying telephone. Upon arriving home I spent the next thirty minutes calling a half dozen farmers in an attempt to locate the hip sling that has helped many a country veterinarians out of a similar jam. I figured I may have left it somewhere along the way at one farm or another. Their groans and puzzled retorts further assured me that I would not locate the sling that night. So off I went, back the seventeen miles to that clever farmer with all the answers.

"We'll have to go up in the hay loft to get the pulleys and rope down and make a sling outta that," said Tony. I wished I hadn't put that idea into his brain an hour or so ago. Good old Tony! I shall never forget standing eighteen feet above the hay loft floor pulling the rope through the pulleys–a device that might make the difference between success and failure in finally delivering this dead calf. Mercifully, the feat was finally accomplished and despite a dead calf the cow did survive!

I gazed at my bloodied watch: 5:15 a.m. I was too cold and too dirty to much care about anything. I cleaned up my instruments as best I could and handed Tony the bill: Twenty seven dollars and fifty cents.

"Wouldja settle for twenty bucks?" he said.

"Yeah, Tony, I just need to get home, I've got a full day in front of me," I said, astounded and rather shocked. I would have never dreamed that such an experience like this as a country vet could shake me into reality so fast–the reality of quibbling over hard-earned bucks in the wee hours of the morning after a cow's life had literally been saved.

I packed my Pandora bag and headed out of the milk house door. My first step out proved to be my last as I slid feet-first down the icy concrete steps into a heap at the bottom. I broke into a hysterical laugh as I picked myself up and collected my instruments which had been scattered in eight directions in the muck.

"Life's got to be easier than this," I muttered to myself as I slammed my bag into the trunk. As Tony nodded a farewell I started my Chevy and muttered a few more choice words to myself, seeing the end of an annoying night finally in sight. But it wasn't to be over yet! I had moved barely fifteen feet with my car when my car's driveshaft thumped a large rock half-buried in the barnyard muck. I limped back into town with a bent driveshaft and a bruised ego. I had little to show for my effort but a dead calf, twenty dollars, more than my share of muck and blood on my face and a crippled car. But we did have a live cow!

And yet, looking back after all this time, those were the precious years of my country practice. The anguish, the simple joys of helping an animal to heal, the blood and even the muck and the smells, are all part of the fabric of being a country veterinarian. Thankfully, there are not that many "Tony's" out there. The satisfaction of helping a farmer in need, his animals and thus, his livelihood, is not easily measured. One does not forget that genuine "Thanks, Doc," or that card in the mail when he hears you are sick or when he finds you're leaving town for the last time. Poignant reminders of what really counts in life. Good, good feelings!

* * * * * * *

A WAGON WHEEL AS BARTER?

Bill Finch, one of the area's most profitable farmers was also one of the county's proudest and most well-respected individuals. But, unfortunately, he was also known for his stinginess. Always on top of the latest news regarding farming changes, new ideas–and ways to save money, he kept up with everything. But in a peculiar sort of way he was an open-minded fellow and listened to his sons, all three of whom were destined to become good farmers in this area as well. No doubt they would inherit the place one day. In addition to a large dairy operation the Finch family produced maple syrup by tapping the many mature trees on their farm. They were good at everything they did and the maple syrup they produced was Grade A, the best anyone could buy with its very light amber color. Many farmers in the area did maple sugaring in winter but none of them had syrup that measured up to the Finch standards.

Bill somehow managed to convince himself of the need to expand his farming operation if his three boys were to continue on there. He was getting older and eventually all three boys would likely marry and have a family of their own. They would need the income. So Bill and his wife decided to "go-for-broke," but only this one time, mind you. They'd go for the latest methods popular at that time and they built what is known as a free-stall operation with its attendant milking parlor. Thus, the dairy cows were housed in a large loafing area of the barn and were fed automatically. A computerized system inputs the animal's number from a tag that is on a chain around its neck and measures out the appropriate amount of grain concentrates according to the animal's production record. Hey, no work, no food!

At milking time, which usually occurs twice daily, the cows follow one after another, like Pavlov's dog, into the milking parlor where machines automatically draw the milk from the cow's udder; and when the milk stream stops the machine turns itself off and falls from the udder. Such is the progress seen nowadays. Gone are most of the small farms where cows are neatly lined up in stanchions waiting for the dairyman to move from one animal to the next until all of them have been relieved of their milk load.

Now, Bill wanted to slowly phase out of his part of the operation and concentrate more on the maple syrup business. He started to clean up the area around their home, make the place tidy and also to no longer hear his wife's nagging about "all that mess around here."

As I was leaving the property one day I noticed a huge old wooden wagon wheel that Bill was about to haul, along with other junk, to the rear of the farm into the woods and be left there for Mother Nature to do her part. That wheel had to be at least seventy five years old. "Hey, Bill, what are you gonna do with that wheel," I said.

"Why, do you want it?"

"Yeah, I could paint it a nice white color and put it by the brick wall in front of the house," I said.

"How about $30.00?"

"Oh, I was going to get some of that maple syrup, too, maybe a pint, okay?"

"That'll be $40.00 total, seein' as I'm givin' you a break on the wheel."

Frank, the oldest son, was nearby working on a machine and overheard the conversation. "Dad, for God's Sake, Doc just stopped by to see how that cow he treated last night was doin'. Give him a break, will ya!"

"Alright, $35 bucks and it's yours!"

"It's a deal," I said. I half-smiled because I knew of his ancestral background.

Just a year later I went to Bill's funeral with the same son standing there at the casket with me. "He was a crusty old man but I loved him and I'll sure miss him," said Frank with tears in his eyes.

Maybe just then I felt the warmth and goodness of that family coming through one final time. Two years later I left that practice and some of those fine people there who were "the salt of the earth." Those were really very good times and very kind, humble people. Memories!

* * * * * * *

WHAT BULL!

Greg and his wife, Mary Elisabeth thought they had hit it big. They were given a "golden parachute" of considerable size as they were told that Greg's position with his company had been eliminated. The company had graciously given him a wonderful severance package. Despite his anger and frustration over this unfortunate happening Greg made the most of it and he and his wife of twenty-five years both had similar thoughts about future plans.

They had saved well, budgeted fastidiously and their nest egg was substantial. They were from similar rural backgrounds and their parents taught them well about saving for a rainy day. And their two adult children were reasonably educated, though still single. Both lived in other states, and had the good fortune of having stable, and good-paying jobs.

This was a perfect time for this enterprising couple to fulfill a longing desire they had discussed many times. They would buy a small farm in the country not far from their urban home. They went the usual route of selling their home after several months of frustration over the lax real estate market in the area. Finding a country place was easy comparatively speaking. They agreed that they would have chickens, a couple of horses and especially some cattle to keep them busy. And keeping food on the table meant that they'd have a substantial vegetable garden and home-raised organic meat, free of all those antibiotics that they'd read about so many times.

They found a place that had some fifteen acres of open land that would serve as a great pasture for newly-acquired bovines. Mary E, as she liked to be called, shopped the weekly cattle sales near their new home and steadily accumulated a mix of beef calves of different ages. And though all of this was a new venture for her she did surprisingly well in haggling for the right prices with some of the old "geezers" at the sales barn who chuckled behind her back about "that city gal over there."

Ultimately, with Greg's approval, Mary E had what she thought was about the right number of animals for their property. The old barn that sat close to the woods on their property would easily hold all of them, with room to spare, in the cold winters of this Minnesota outback. The garden would have to wait until next year.

But a few months later a rather strange appearance in three of their cattle caused them some concern. They called in the local veterinarian, a gruff older man–smart, to-the-point, but not given to much small talk. It seemed to them that the three cattle were not looking as they usually do; something was not quite right but Greg didn't know what it was. He had heard about a situation called bloat that occurs occasionally in cattle. Greg was quite concerned and called Mary E out of the house to the fence where two of the three animals were standing, chewing their cuds contentedly. Dr. Martin, after briefly checking over two of the three animals was already soaping up his long shoulder-length rubber sleeve and after telling Greg to halter the animal he inserted his arm deep into a cow's pelvic cavity. Unusual for this crusty old man, he gave out a "whoop" and then a knowing smile.

"What's goin' on, Doc? What are ya not tellin' me? Is it serious?"

"Yep, serious alright, how many cows you got here anyway?"

"Seventeen; why, am I gonna lose one?"

"Nope, you're gonna gain one–this one's pregnant!"

"C'mon, that couldn't be," said Greg, "These animals are all fenced in. I spent two months to build the fence myself."

Further examination of the other two animals verified Dr. Martin's comment–all three were pregnant. Mary E was embarrassed and then recalled how the old men at the sale guffawed when she unknowingly bought a bull calf. One day she'd get back at them all and let them know she was no rooky in this "farming business." But, looking at it another way–she now quickly regained her composure and started to smile contentedly; she was getting three more animals that didn't cost her a cent!

* * * * * * *

THEN THERE WERE THREE

The afternoon whistle signaled the end of a day of drudgery at the travel trailer manufacturing plant where Mike Sanchez worked as a supervisor. He couldn't get to his car fast enough. Pat, his young wife told him in the morning that her due date had arrived and she felt very strange about him going to work at the plant that particular day. She was expecting a boy and the sonogram showed the little guy to be bigger than she had ever expected. How she could ever go through this delivery the natural way, she constantly fretted. She vowed that she would never again allow another pregnancy to consume so much of her life. Each day that past month had been pure hell... false labor pains, spotting, real labor pains... she never knew what was in store from one day to the next.

Ironically, Stacy, their Golden Retriever mix was also pregnant. Stacy bopped around the house seemingly delighted to be bringing into the world a replica of herself, maybe two, maybe a whole bunch. She'd love and lick them every waking moment while they would be nursing or just snuggling by her side. Stacy was a very predictable pooch; always outside by the door, waiting to come in for a love pat or for a drink of water. But neither Mike nor Pat knew that Stacy was pregnant. There weren't any suitors in the immediate neighborhood to their knowledge. At least, none hung around the house!

Later in the evening Mike saw it first... a spot of blood the size of a quarter on the floor near the sink in the kitchen. He asked Pat rather nervously if there was a problem "in that department"... had she noticed anything different? She hadn't checked in the past ten minutes but all was okay then. Mike, a first time father-to-be and "worry-wart" of sorts, panicked and called the obstetrician's office. The doctor's receptionist arranged for them to meet with the doctor as soon as they were able to get to the hospital.

From there on it was pure pandemonium; Poor Mike forgot to put his shoes on and only after pulling up to the hospital entrance with Pat did he realize his error. He had only his slippers on, and under his coat, his shortie pajamas.

The obstetrician handled the entire situation with a calming voice. All was okay after a brief exam. Mike assured Pat that it would all work out fine and they headed home. A restful evening was all they were hoping for.

It was when they arrived home that Mike added embarrassment to his already flustered self-image. As he turned the corner into the kitchen he heard the faint slurping of the new mother licking her puppies... one after another in what seemed a practiced regimen... first the spotted one, next the brindle-marked male and finally the smaller black one. Stacy seemed utterly content. She was oblivious to Mike and Pat's presence.

How could they both have missed all the tell-tale signs of a canine mother-to-be: the increase in appetite, the unquenchable thirst and the pacing... the constant pacing, starting just a few days ago?

Next time, if there ever was going to be a next time, Mike would be the wiser.

He and Pat would know when to call Pat's doctor, and know when his unpredictable dog would grace the family with a litter of pups. And certainly he'd know that shortie pajamas and slippers are not the dress-of-the day in the doctor's office.

* * * * * * *

REFLECTIONS

Stuart, a local vet in the neighboring farming community, was questioning why he got into medicine in the first place; it seems that every farmer, horseman and dairyman he came across had his own opinion as to how or what to treat an animal with. And it really bothered him. It was frustrating him to the point of his just wanting to stay home and get into the wood working projects that he so dearly loved. After all, he made some gorgeous cherry cabinets for his wife, he had all the woodworking machines and tools that he'd ever need and he'd love not having to run out in the middle of the night to treat some sick cow that should have been treated while the sun was still shining. Maybe he could get some sleep like a normal person and get up and languish in his shop amongst the shavings and aroma of the pine and cherry wood that he felt so comfortable around.

I had learned, from many years in practice, to just close my ears to it all, but still listen "with one ear open" for the sometimes logical things that were brought up by clients as well as the humorous stories that were sure to follow. And I sincerely hoped that Stu would settle down and fully accept the profession that he had chosen and was really good at. I recall him relating how, after performing a Caesarian section on a Holstein cow, his wife called and told him that he'd better be home soon because a little girl down the street had just called. She had a gerbil that had a tumor on its eye. The girl, only eight years old, was distraught because it was her first and only animal. The mother said she wouldn't allow a dog or cat because she was allergic, and besides, "they're smelly and they lose a lot of hair."

Stu got right down to business when he arrived home–told his wife that dinner can wait a bit and this little girl's gerbil was really important to her. He had the heart of a giant even though physically he was a little guy, barely five feet-three inches tall. And he had a slight limp caused by a childhood case of polio. I often wondered how he could handle an eighteen hundred pound uncooperative cow or, for that matter, even a small horse. But with his determination, once he set his mind to it he could do anything. And this gerbil was just another problem that he'd handle just fine.

"No big deal" he'd say, "Just dilute the anesthetic by ten-to-one ratio, titrate it out precisely, and you're all set." He had done this in another practice and learned that some things are not always in the book. The surgery went well and to this day he's reminded by the child's mother that the gerbil lived its life happily ever after and the eye itself was not harmed, only the upper lid remained a bit uneven.

Stu, his wife Joanne, and my wife and I spent many an evening playing cards after dinner and relating to some of the silly things in our practices that almost made us roll on the floor in laughter. Then, I recalled, there was Fred, the local dairyman who wrapped his calf's swollen lower front leg in a sauerkraut wrap because he'd heard it would bring the swelling down overnight. Four days later he ran out of sauerkraut and called me. Upon inspection the poor calf had a broken leg and sauerkraut would not have helped–ever. We needed to put a cast on the leg and, being a youngster, the animal's leg would heal well.

And then there was Walt, with his German accent;

"You haf to see vhat I found in za voods, Doc. Zis animal vill be famous vun day!" Walt was a former factory worker, married a German girl in the village and decided to buy a small farm. Only a few acres, but enough land and a barn in which he could putter around. So when I arrived we went out to the barn to see this magical wonder. It was an undersized calf, weighed about thirty-five pounds, staring directly at us.

"Vatch zis, Doc," he said, "As soon as I get 'glose to him, he chumps up like crazy, goes in bik circles and falls down. Zen I touch him and he starts all ofer again. Vhat du you sink? ," he said with a confident smile, his pleasant German accent causing me to chuckle openly.

Walt had been out in his woods looking for mushrooms for his wife. She had trained him which ones to look for and which ones to avoid because some are deadly poison. He became rather good at it. On his way home with his mushrooms he found this small calf, hidden in a deeply isolated area of the woods, apparently abandoned by its mother, something that does not happen very often. He carried the animal home, fed it a commercial calf-starter from a nipple pail for two days and thought nothing else of it. Then, the next morning the little "circus act" started and Walt smiled, thinking he was onto something big.

Walter, of course, never heard about Circling Disease, or Listeriosis, a bacterial disease that invades the body of mammals and occasionally the brain, causing permanent damage and, in the case of this little calf, a disoriented kind of circling. The prognosis on something like this is very poor and the animal will eventually die. I advised Walter about this poor beast's future and he, being a kind sort, wanted to immediately put it down, which I did.

Walter had a great sense of humor and he smiled, even laughed a little bit later on.

"You know, I chust yesterday told za vife she'd vud have to start a new little bank account to keep track of za dollars coming in vhen ve take him to za carnival next year. Oh, vell, I buy her a nice chicken for za pot and she vill be okay. Vhat do you sink, Doc, No?"

* * * * * * *

ANOTHER OFF DAY

Mr. Cal Amity called to say he needed to bring his dog Loco in for a checkup and the usual vaccinations. When he showed up the receptionists thought it wasn't the same dog they'd seen before. His face was swollen grotesquely and he looked very downtrodden and sad. In the exam room I noticed all the stubble around his nose. It was then that Mr. Amity mentioned that poor Loco tangled with a porcupine a few days ago.

Cal's mail lady, Doris, had brought a package to his door and noticed the poor wretch with all the quills sticking out. She advised him about the shortcut to all those needless vet bills and true to her "professional" advice he clipped all the quills to about one eighth inch long. Needless to say this didn't solve the problem and the dog had to be admitted, placed under a short-acting anesthetic and the quills pulled out, one at a time.

It was later that day that Ms. Bea Zarr came by with her beautiful calico cat, Biscuit, for some serious consultation about behavioral problems her kitty was into. Seems she was urinating regularly on a new white carpet upstairs in the house. I advised her that she had three choices: have the cat spayed, get a yellow carpet or take her to the new office in town, Katy's Kitty Kounselling Service. She grew furious with me and walked out. I chuckled to myself knowing that, as usual, any attempt at advice would fall on deaf ears.

She had called a week earlier to inquire of any male calico cats they may be available for stud service. I am a lover of calico cats. It is well known that all true calico-colored cats are females. Only once have I encountered a three-colored male cat but that one was gray, orange and white rather than black, orange and white. She immediately informed me that she took a genetics course at the local community college and that she was getting into the cat breeding business. She had great aspirations about creating a new pure strain of calicos. She even had a new genus and species envisioned; Felis catus, variety; Calicotus carolus, in honor of her dear friend Carol, another breeder. I thought Carol might have to wait a long time to receive that infamous recognition.

The rest of the day went rather uneventfully. On the way home I passed Arnie's place, a veterinary practitioner who started there a few years ago and a nice colleague. Standing next to her bright red pickup was Bea Zarr with her new addition, a tri-colored baby Nubian goat. I felt sorry for Arnie. I had the car in cruise control but instinctively I smiled and stepped on the gas. On some days just driving home can be so very comforting.

* * * * * * *

AMONG THE BLESSED

I was fourteen years old then, going to do a small job for my Mother up near the house. I was in the barn and heading for the big sliding door to the right but I suddenly remembered that I needed a saw and a hammer for the job. So, instead I turned left to go up through the stable and horse barn to get what I needed. I walked no farther than fifteen feet when I heard a thunderous roar outside. I turned, saw more daylight than usual and went to the big door, opened it and saw a frightening spectacle: the silo, that majestic wood and steel tower, some fifty feet tall, that self-assigned guardian of all the buildings on the farm, and visible for miles around, lay completely prostrate on the ground, a mass of tangled metal hoops and wooden staves. How could such an important and dignified structure be reduced to rubble in an instant by a transient, indifferent and insulting blast of wind? Moments later, I recovered from the fright that overwhelmed me and I half-smiled. Had I turned the other way, I realized right then where I might lay at that very moment. I was very much alive and extremely lucky. Looking back days later, I thought: I am Among the Blessed.

* * *

Some years later, many years later, my new bride and I left the church, and rain from every direction unmercifully pelted us and all of our well-wishers. Our honeymoon trip to Florida was about to begin!

We wing our way to Florida, as planned many months ago; we arrived and it was raining there as well but, no matter, we were on our honeymoon. Even the patrolman who pulled us over commented rather sadly about the incessant rain.

"Move on," he said finally, after a brief lecture, "and don't get stopped again, okay? You're gettin' a break from me. I was on a honeymoon once myself."

Key Biscayne was such a tantalizing place. The blueness of the water seemed unmatched by any place I had ever been, but then again at that stage of my life I hadn't really been to that many tantalizing places!

My bride wanted to take a nap but I would prefer a swim so I readied myself and I walked easily to the beach. Arriving in moments, I was instantly perplexed... befuddled, a better word; the beach was totally empty... devoid of all the beach-combers, the strollers, and of course, all the swimmers. What was going on? But that was okay... more privacy for me, a poor swimmer not wanting to be embarrassed. I merely wanted to take a dip in that heavenly sea, so inviting, and so very, very blue! No more than ten minutes in the water and I heard a faint whir, weird and strange and coming from behind and to the left and quickly growing louder. I turned to my left and less than five yards away a giant school of fish, sunfish perhaps, took to the air. By the hundreds, seemingly, they flew through the air in an arc of immeasurable dimension only to land per-haps twenty five feet forward of where I was standing. I was completely paralyzed with fear. Perhaps instinctively I made for the shore, frightened by a sight I had never and may never again witness.

As I reached the sandy beach I noticed an elderly couple sitting in folding chairs up on the break wall. "Did you see that?" I yelled, shaking from head to toe. Evidently not hearing me they looked at me with that puzzled look but with no response. Again, I yelled: "Did you see that... those fish flying through the air?"

With a quick wave of the arm he pointed to a sign that, clearly, I had missed completely. It said: BEACH CLOSED: SHARK WARNING. "Oh, my God," I retorted," I never saw it."

To which he replied: "I figured you were probably one of those kooks that never listen to anything anyway."

Thanks a lot, I thought!

Shakily, I headed towards my hotel. I remember still trembling all the way back. When my bride saw me she said, with fear evident on her beautiful face; "What's the matter; you're white as a ghost?"

I believe I even felt a little pale. No one would ever know if indeed my life was in imminent danger, or even if a shark had me in his sights or olfactory range. My wife might quite possibly have had to leave Key Biscayne as a new widow. And I felt that, once again, I am Among the Blessed.

* * *

Exhausted but content after delivering live triplet lambs from Enos Barker's ewe I got a reprieve from my wife and I took the free time of that slow day to work on the cabin that I was building. It was a mere seven miles from home and en route I stopped by his farm to make certain the little lambs were doing well enough considering their tortuous entry into this world.

Working with my hands has for me always been a gift from Above. It has always given me great satisfaction; I knew exactly what I wanted to tackle that day and there was a lot on my agenda. The location of my cabin was far from any natural gas lines so we were limited to an all-electric supply for heat, cooking and hot water. Having just installed the water heater myself and accepting the expense of electric heat I wanted to minimize the heat loss from the cabin by heavily insulating the crawl space below the floor. Sadly, there was a lot of standing water in that crawl space which I was quite unhappy about. I slipped on my rubber boots, newly acquired just a week ago. I pushed the foil-covered insulation batting through the trap door opening and proceeded to methodically tack it up between all the floor joists. As I was coming into the last section I was standing in eight inches of water to finish the last stretch of insulation. Unaware of the three-hundred amp cable in that space I squeezed the handle of the stapler. A deafening sound and a ball of fire shot out in front of me. I had penetrated the cable with a staple. I do not recall falling down but I dropped the staple gun and, paralyzed with fear, I quickly exited the crawl space. I lay on the cabin's kitchen floor for an unknown amount of time, wondering if I was truly still alive in this mortal world. My new veterinary boots had actually saved my life. Or, was it really the boots?

Once again, I consider myself Among the Blessed.

* * *

I lay in the hospital bed, the pain of a long abdominal incision starting to sear through me like a hot knife. I had just been returned to a semi-private room from Intensive Care and I was ready to start the recovery process and to be back again in the everyday world outside. With a week of intravenous nourishment, fine hospital care and the well wishes of the kind staff at that hospital, I felt eager to leave. I was grateful to hear at least a guarded prognosis and to go home again and be with all its familiar aromas. The warm surroundings of home, the telephone calls and cards from concerned friends would buoy my spirits and usher me out of my depression.

And so now, exactly two years after that surgery and a telephone call from my wonderful attending surgeon, Dr. Lawrence Koep, I again smile gratefully for the very encouraging results of test after test affirming my good health and the apparent absence of any serious internal disease process.

I ask myself... what is it that allows me, just another human being, to be so very fortunate? We all see youngsters in St. Jude's or other hospitals, many with terminal cancer or other chronic and often fatal maladies. Such innocent lives; what have they done to merit this tragic situation? I hope someday we all have the answer.

But now, and one more time, I say: Thank You, Lord, I am truly Among the Blessed.

* * * * * * *

MITTENS

I've always had a love for cats, those mysterious, independent, sultry, vain bundles of sass and aplomb. It has been said that "Cats allow you to live with them in their home!" How very true!

I have especially loved the calico-colored variety; over the years we've had several cats, as well as dogs, but calicos and our family have had a love affair with one another. I've seen them with the most unusual arrangement of colors, sometimes with a black circle of hair around one eye, another with a patch of orange on the front of the chest resembling the number seven.

When we moved into our new home we had our "Benji-type" dog but soon we were out shopping for a calico kitten. We were very fussy, too! We preferred a short-haired female since one of our daughters seemed to have an allergy of sorts in her early years. We found her... our favorite color and we named her Mittens. Our dog, Fuzzy, after a few days of trial acceptance, finally learned that cats are indeed unique... never to be intimidated by the likes of a dog or anything else for that matter. Mittens asserted her rights and independence from day one and knew what a "hiss" was for and how to use it. Her size and her attitude grew without falter and within three months she assumed her position in the family "pecking order" as though she had been bequeathed as the Queen of the House.

We lived in a rural area and our neighbor had a Staffordshire terrier. He was big and he was aptly named "Schreck." Now, Schreck was never a "Mister-Nice-Guy;" he usually stayed home but on occasion he'd wander into our backyard and growl when first seeing one of us adults. He wasn't particularly the engaging type, never backed away when challenged and seemed to dare us to shoo him off the property. Other neighbors as well knew of him and his questionable manner. He had killed one of the Smith's cats and because of that his reputation was sullied even before we had any encounter with him.

On one occasion I was in a trench covering a newly-laid water line and Schreck stood over the edge of the trench growling at me down below. I yelled at him, to no avail and then I finally pitched my shovel toward him. Not in the least scared, he grabbed the shovel and dragged it some fifteen feet before giving it up. One of our other neighbors, knowing I was a veterinarian, told the owner that he should have the dog neutered; "Nah, he wouldn't be a dog anymore!" he quipped. Schreck and he seemed to be meant for each other.

Our Mittens finally had to be declawed because of the major damage she caused to our new sofa and soft chair... a move I have regretted ever since. Declawed cats lose their ability to climb and for that reason they should be kept inside at all times away from danger, no exception. That was our intention, but not Mittens'. We took every step to assure ourselves that she would not get outdoors...ever !

On occasion she'd try to follow the dog out but we were there to thwart that attempt every time. What we did not expect was Mittens' determination to explore, as all cats are wont to do. She'd sit on the window sill of the family room contentedly most of the time. But inside of her brain lurked a curiosity–the curiosity of a cat... all cats. On September 7th of a Labor Day weekend Mittens decided that she would put her curiosity to a test and secretly leaped up to the partially opened upper sash of a window and jumped outside to the patio. Some time later we heard her cries and went to retrieve her. As soon as she heard the door opening she ran "like there was no tomorrow." She was not about to be captured and be returned to her "prison" inside. We searched for hours and finally gave up for a time intending to resume the search later.

After lunch we had planned to leave for a parade in the next village, but first we needed to find Mittens. Suddenly, we heard a large *meow* and ran to the front porch. There was Mittens, dirty, droopy with tail dragging behind her. She had been injured, how seriously I was about to find out. Picking her up I immediately discovered a totally limp tail, the result of separation of the bones of the tail. Her hair was matted and she was a mess, with bloody scrapes and missing patches of hair on her rear parts.

Immediately we drove to the animal hospital and began intravenous fluid therapy and cleansed her rear parts as delicately as possible. The parade was now a secondary event for us on that day; after several hours we just went home, distraught and feeling the pain of guilt. In the end we needed to amputate Mittens' tail... something that made us harbor guilt feelings for the rest of her life. Additionally, she had suffered damage to the nerves under the rear spine area that permanently caused incontinence. For eight years we, at home or our technicians at the hospital, manually emptied her bladder and bowels daily. We dearly loved that kitty and we did what we had to do to make her more comfortable. We never had words with our neighbor but we just knew that Schreck was the culprit behind this tragedy. Needless to say, they were not the most loved people in our neighborhood.

* * * * * * *

CHARLIE AND THE CURRANT PIE

When little Charlie came into the animal hospital he was wrapped in a blanket; not that it was cold... he was just unable to walk in under his own power. It all started at the beginning of a vacation for his owners, Mr. and Mrs. William Gillespie.

They started telling the story, fully emotionally composed, but within five minutes Mrs. Gillespie started sobbing uncontrollably. Then the story came out, with every minute detail, even including the stopover at a Tastee Freeze just before Charlie's accident.

The little guy, a Dachshund mix, always made it a point while travelling in their car to sit between them, his chin resting comfortably on Mrs. Gillespie's ample left thigh. But as the miles rolled on the little fellow would become a bit bored and would get up and methodically make a leap to the top of the seat-back; from there he would easily leap to the blanketed rear seat and snooze for the balance of the journey. This was his routine, no matter where they went. They were a retired couple and travelled frequently with their faithful companion beside them.

But now Charlie was getting a little older, like the rest of us. In fact, he now rather hesitated to make the jump. Sometimes he would just give up and lie back down, only to attempt the jump an hour or so later. But this time he made the effort and almost made it to the top of the seat-back. Almost.

He fell backward this time, something he'd never done before. He let out a sharp yelp and whined enough so that Mrs. Gillespie stroked his head and said "Poor, poor Charlie, huh?" He lay for a moment and then tried briefly to position himself the way he usually did when reclining between them. He made no effort at all this time to straighten his torso and re-arrange his legs.

At that point the dear lady noticed the wetness of the car seat, something that Charlie would never allow to happen to himself. Mrs. Gillespie motioned to her husband: "Bill, pull over, will you! Something's happened to Charlie!"

After pulling over to the side of the highway Bill noticed that the poor dog was paralyzed in his rear parts. Frightened by this bizarre occurrence, the Gillespies searched out an animal hospital in a little village in central New York State. They inquired at a nearby U.S. Post Office and were directed to one only two miles away. They were very concerned and prepared for the worst. After thorough examination and multiple X-rays by the friendly veterinarian the news was not good.

When Charlie had fallen backward his protruding spine made harsh, direct contact with a seat belt buckle, the one that his master didn't secure after stopping to get ice cream at the Tastee Freeze. The impact of landing in the position he had fallen caused almost immediate paralysis. X-rays had shown that no bones were broken; the impact caused severe bruising and edema of the soft tissue immediately surrounding the spinal cord and although not visible there was likely some bleeding into adjacent tissue as well.

Charlie was admitted to the animal hospital with a guarded prognosis. The distraught owners agreed to leave him with Dr. Samuels with the understanding that there would be intensive treatment as needed, and regular contact with the Gillespies. It was the first time Charlie had been in an animal hospital in over a year and he too seemed frightened. The look on his face hinted fear and anxiety.

For the next three days Dr. Samuels and his staff administered intensive treatment, steroids, intravenous fluids, diuretics–fine care by all standards. But Charlie was not responding at all. There was no sign whatsoever of any change in his condition. Totally distraught Bill and Fran Gillespie made a decision to abandon any further vacation plans and came back that same day with Charlie to our facility in western New York. They had been clients for years. I feared the worst, considering the intense treatments he had already been subjected to. Bill started to quiver, holding back tears as best he could and perhaps even contemplating the worst. I tried to divert my eyes toward the wall.

I explained that given all the intense care that Charlie had received it might be a thought to attack the problem from a different perspective. I had just finished my extensive course work and subsequent certification as a veterinary acupuncturist. Would they be willing to consider that approach? What could they lose? It was my first case to utilize my training in that specialty and I would give it my all. All those several hundred acupuncture points were still very fresh in my mind. Still, I feared failure, to a degree. There are many, many skeptics out there and I had to... wanted to, disprove their skepticism.

The rest is history. Using an advanced method rather than" dry-needling," I treated Charlie daily with electro-acupuncture. For two days there was no response at all. Fear set in! But, on the third day the tip of Charlie's tail would "wiggle" a little. Two days later more of it showed movement. And, there was a slight, very slight increase in muscle tone, and strength in his rear legs. From there forward there was at a one-to-three-day interval, a gradual but visible improvement in Charlie. Even his demeanor changed. Maybe it changed for the better because he knew us, trusted us. One never knows.

Charlie was a patient at my animal hospital for a little over three weeks. He was "my little experiment" and I felt so very confident. In this case acupuncture worked and it worked beautifully. Not all cases respond like Charlie's. Some cases do not respond at all. In fact, for me acupuncture was unsuccessful. The partial leg paralysis I have had for several years showed no improvement after a dozen treatments. But, unlike injectable or oral medications the positive aspect of acupuncture is this; if there is no improvement there also are no side effects, no nausea, no secondary issues, some of which can be very, very serious. Unfortunately one can never predict which way things will go.

Weeks later, this charming couple came by with Charlie to say "Thank You" and to let him demonstrate how well he got around–evidently quite happy, tail wagging with familiarity. It was then that I mentioned, after a brief chat about ice cream, Tastee Freeze and other goodies that my family and I would be off on a trip for ten days. I offered to let them stop by at our home while we were gone to harvest some over-ripe currants from a bush in our back yard. In my busy practice I had neglected to harvest them. Unpicked, they would soon rot. They knew what currants were, they really liked them, and readily accepted my offer.

It didn't end there. Four days after returning from our vacation Mrs. Gillespie stopped by at the office and asked to see me for a quick moment. The staff hadn't noticed the box in her hand. She had brought me a currant pie–homemade, of course. When I attempted to politely refuse, she chuckled: "Doc, I've got two more of these same pies at home, all from that one currant bush!"

How thankful and gracious these clients were. Though not a usual thing, this was one of my many rewards of being an animal doctor.

* * * * * * *

Rollin' Along With Steam

From our kitchen, my wife had just heard the familiar "whoo-whoo" of the locomotive as the train rolled into town on a Sunday afternoon. The Attica Railroad, now a familiar tourist train with its bright orange engine and three passenger cars had just returned from its distant terminus some 12 miles north. It was there that the engine was shunted off onto a side track, the three passenger cars pushed forward, and now the engine with its three tourist cars would be back in town.

This little railroad is listed among the Registers of familiar tourist trains across the USA. It has been in existence for many years, initially travelling some 25 miles to another town world famous for its prison. The prison, Attica, holds many of the "lifers," as they're known. Among them is Son of Sam, guilty of several killings on his murderous rampage many years ago and now looking from the inside out until he draws his final breath. Others, too numerous to mention, all bide their time waiting for their inevitable day of reckoning or of meeting their Maker.

The train's engineer, Manley Jackson, was on duty that day. He chose to work weekends because he was also a dairy farmer. In fact, farming was his livelihood, but to add a little color to his life he put in an application eight years earlier to be the train's main engineer. He loved that engineer's job, probably a lot more than dairy farming, and it was a heck of a lot easier. He had loved trains ever since boyhood and even had stored the old Lionel model toys in his attic. The pay, as the engineer, while not great, gave him little more than pocket change as well as a way to replenish his coffers of chewing tobacco.

Manley had a real knack for storytelling. Actually, he should have been back in one of the tourist cars giving his version of a shootout that he experienced in a small town not far from Attica a few years before he took on the responsibility of being the train's main engineer.

Manley relied on me, his veterinarian, to take care of his animals when they got sick... a mule, eighteen dairy cows and a couple of "beefers." He was such an easy-going fellow. He loved to keep me in stitches with one story after another as I worked on a cow or calf that was sick or needed attention. Nothing bothered Manley, not even my ultra-loud scream on the day he invited me and my year-old son to sit in the cab of his locomotive as we were about to steam north some 12 miles away to the train's northern-most destination.

Manley had just said: "Now just sit yourself down on that there seat, Doc–the best seat in the house, while I build up a little more steam on Old Nellie here. It'll only be a couple of minutes yet and we'll get agoin'."

What Manly didn't tell me was that the steam pipe coming from the engine's boiler was tight against the left wall of the engine. As I jostled to get my happy little guy situated properly on my lap my left leg grazed that scorching hot steam pipe. Manley never heard me; he just kept on yakking about all the things that made that engine so mighty. Like a bolt of lightning I jumped off the stool, my son Rob in my arms!

Manley had a look of shock on his face. "Whatsa matter, Doc, somethin' bite ya?"

I was glad it was me and not my son. I sported a water blister twelve inches long and three inches wide on my left thigh for almost two weeks. I showed it to him four days later at the farm and he just laughed like crazy, totally unaware of the excruciating pain that steam pipe inflicted on me.

Years went by, Manley passed into The Netherworld and his widow managed to keep a few animals around, mostly for companionship, I felt. When I was back at the farm one day she produced the page of the newspaper showing his obituary. Proudly, she had written his "profession" as Head Railroad Engineer and secondarily as: "farmer."

"He would have loved that," she said with proudly raised chin and a smile. "It was his life!" Simple pleasures.

Those were "the olden days," with small and insignificant happenings at the time but no less memorable. It was a lot different then, the years when I was catering to the little farms, their owners trying to scratch out a living in the back country of western New York.

* * * * * * *

Assert Yourself, Young Man

Having been brought up on a large dairy farm with a couple teams of draft horses was a good experience for us kids. Those gentle "plugs," as my Dad called them, were anything but a challenge. Billy and Sally were the gentlest animals one could ever imagine. If you stood next to Billy's face he'd nuzzle you or nibble your flannel shirt. It was as though he wanted to just say something to you but couldn't form the words in that big bulky mouth of his. Surely, he had a few thoughts to convey if only his brain would allow it!

When my Dad finished planting corn at dusk he would just unhook the team from the corn planter and slap one of them on the rump, say "Giddap" and they'd head home from the field by themselves. They'd still be hooked together with the neck yoke up front and the traces behind while he stayed back to burn the empty fertilizer bags. They knew where their next meal came from and they'd head home by themselves to the stables, often well over a half mile away. Oddly, one day when he finally got home he could not find the team he had sent on ahead. As it turns out they were out of sight at the backside of the barns by another set of doors. They instinctively ended up there because on the previous day Dad had given them a treat at that door after they had pulled a big clumsy machine out of the shed for him.

Now, living at the riding stables at the university was quite another experience for me. Draft horses and polo ponies are about as alike as apples and bananas. The temperament of the latter is something else to behold! It is rather a kind of "mind thing," an instinct of sorts, something one apparently either has or doesn't have—something only an experienced equestrian understands or, perhaps it is a natural part of one's makeup.

I initially dreaded my new duty at the stables; I'd never mucked out polo ponies or any other sleek riding horses, for that matter. I quickly learned that they, with little exception, were often quite high-strung, edgy, often easily scared. Upon my walking into the first box stall occupied by a beautiful chestnut-colored gelding, I should have known that muscle-rippled brute had sized me up in seconds. I was a rank amateur and he knew it as soon as he sensed the fear that pulsed through my very being.

I picked myself up from the straw-covered box stall floor before I fully realized that I had been leveled by a lightning-like blast of his left hind leg. Scared but unhurt I left and asked my buddy, Joe, to finish with that stall while I moved to a "safer" box stall. The next morning I unthinkingly entered that same box stall, probably even more scared than the previous day. One more time this overly-confident chestnut gelding leveled me with a precision swipe as though he had practiced the maneuver overnight.

Joe taught me something that day: animals are very quick to sense fear and they do what they need to do to protect themselves. He taught me to cover that fear offensively. On the third day we both entered the box stall at the same time. Joe took over. He brazenly took three brisk steps, smacked the horse hard on the rump and at the very same moment let loose with a barrage of swear words that were probably heard at the women's dorm a half mile away! The horse quivered, pulled back his ears and trembled. The rest took care of itself. I never had a problem with any polo pony after that. It was not as though they all needed an authority figure; nor did they need physical action taken; they needed to sense who is in charge and I suspect most horsemen instinctively know that.

I established my country practice as a mixed animal practitioner but the bulk of my work at that time was with dairy cattle, sheep and the occasional pig or beef animal. On occasion I would do some equine work but a veterinarian not far from my own practice area loved working with horses much more than with cattle and I sometimes referred those clients to him. That way we were both happy. We each knew what we were best at!

* * * * * * *

CRAZY MAN KENNEDY

"Damn near killed myself " was the first thing Frank Kennedy said to me and father as he rolled the old Buick into the garage for an oil change at Kennedy's Garage two days after the Fourth of July holiday. My father knew exactly what he was referring to. Kennedy had a bi-wing Cessna airplane that he flew regularly when business at the garage was slow as well as on holidays in the summer months.

"You damn fool, you're gonna kill yourself one of these days," scolded his wife Mabel. She was content to stay at home in her own world, devoid of the craziness of Frank. She had no idea of some of the tricks he pulled off in his plane. She had never even ridden in it. He'd do barrel rolls, near stalls—you name it. That plane was his life.

"Greasin' up cars and fixin' brakes has its limits in enjoyment," he'd say. Or, "The old lady's usually too tired for anything else," a statement that could have meant many things but when accompanied by that boyish smile it gave clear meaning to my Dad.

Back to the Fourth of July; we were out in the field by our house back East having a grand time lighting and shooting off firecrackers. We had pin wheels, sky rockets, wing rockets, some with little parachutes attached, and some with a million color displays. And, of course, the occasional dud that got us really mad. We'd run like crazy through the corn rows guessing where they'd land... all six of us, to see who'd maybe come up with a prize parachute. If one of the girls got there first we'd yank it away saying: "They're not for you sissies," and run off with the bootie.

Tommy, my brother and the quietest one in the family, matter-of-factly said: "You can have Thanksgiving and all the punkin' pie you can eat but there's nothin' like shootin' off fire-crackers!"

To this day he talks it up like it was just last year that we all got together, and with my father yelling: "Be careful, I can't afford to take you to the hospital

So when we heard that plane flying overhead we lost all interest in fireworks. It came upon us with a deafening roar but, despite that it was really a treat to watch the pilot doing those dips and dives as he came near. Bi-wing planes always intrigued us. They were kind of a novelty to us kids. How Mr. Kennedy knew just where our farm was, was a mystery in itself.

Back in those days not all public roads out in our neck of the woods even had names; many were just dirt roads. Frequently you'd see a cow pie in the middle of the road somewhere and that was when the nearest way to take cows to the pasture was along a public road. People seemed kinder, less rushed then; they'd accept their fate and amble along behind us in their cars, not wanting to scatter the animals off into the bush by tooting the horn. Only once did a man, apparently in a rush or late for work, get impatient with these lazy, ambling bovines. He blasted on his horn and most of the cows scattered–

but not all. He yelled out of the window to no avail and our poor Brownie just refused to move over. Perhaps she had a hearing problem, no one knows. Then he got brave and nudged his front bumper against the beast. Instantly, she favored the one hind leg, but then he bumped her again. This time she hobbled off to the side of the road as best she could and he moved on slowly through the rest of the scattered herd.

That evening when we went to the pasture to retrieve the cows we found Brownie lying next to the gate, probably having stayed there the entire day. The veterinarian came, looked at the leg and told my dad that she had a broken leg; she was sent to the butcher the next day. Brownie was one of our favorites; she was so docile and we would think of her as almost a pet with her brindle-colored hide and big dark eyes. Even her milk seemed to taste a little richer.

Now, when the mailman came we knew in an instant of his arrival by the cloud of dust he kicked up as he flew around the countryside in his trusty black Hudson sedan, trying to get his route finished before four p.m. Mr. Tillson and Kennedy were drinking buddies. Both had some good stories and laughs discussing the good times they had "back in the old days." So it was no surprise at all when Tillson came up to the house to deliver a package that he shared with my dad about the close calls "that crazy fool Kennedy" had through the years with his plane! "I rode with him once and that was enough," he said; "that guy's nuts!"

That was the year Frank did a "dipsy-doodle" with his Cessna on the Fourth of July in the sky right by our house. He was no higher than thirty-five feet from the ground and then he roared off into the sunset.

I'll bet he was laughing his head off. What he didn't know was that just ten feet above his plane were two high-tension power lines. He had no idea they were there and he had gone directly under them. A bit higher and he would have been history! Now *that* would have been a fireworks display that nobody else would have loved more than us innocent kids!

Life goes on...
Frank Kennedy is gone now
and Mr. Tillson is still delivering mail
in the High Beyond.
But the picture of Mr. Kennedy
in his plane doing tricks lives on
in our glorious memories
some seventy years later.

* * * * * *

About The Author

Born to German immigrant parents, Robert Hirt is one of six children–three boys, and three girls–who were reared in a rural farming environment in the Hudson Valley of New York State.

As a young, energetic kid, he wanted to learn about almost everything, but especially science and biology. He did well scholastically and his parents encouraged pursuing a college education. He rather enjoyed being around animals on their dairy farm. In addition to cows they had chicken, pigs, draft horses, cats, as well as a dog and a goat. He excelled in his university studies and was accepted at Cornel University, where he completed a degree program for Doctor of Veterinary Medicine. For him it was the perfect choice

Earning his degree as Doctor of Veterinary Medicine at Cornell University he spent many years as a country practitioner, serving the needs of area farmers.

Since retirement he derives considerable pleasure in recounting many episodes that brought him, sometimes frustrating, but more often satisfying experiences of having been a country vet.

He presently resides in Chandler, Arizona with Patricia, his wife of forty seven years.

Manufactured by Amazon.ca
Acheson, AB